"

SEEING A GIRL IN THE RIGHT SHOE IS LIKE RIDING IN
A CAR WHEN A GREAT SONG COMES ON THE RADIO,
AND YOU GET A LITTLE TINGLE DOWN YOUR SPINE.

STEVE MADDEN

"

On the cover: Steven by Steve Madden *Revolvir Pump*
—Designed exclusively for DSW—

THIS BOOK IS THE VERY SERIOUS OBSESSION OF:

_____

SHOE LOVER

ISBN: 978-1-118-67422-2 (paper)
ISBN: 978-1-118-78220-0 (ebk)
ISBN: 978-1-118-78221-7 (ebk)

Printed in the United States of America

10 9 8 7 6 5 4 3 2

DO YOU SPEAK SHOE LOVER?

STYLE AND STORIES FROM INSIDE DSW

LINDA MEADOW AND THE SHOE LOVERS AT DSW

WILEY

The Carrie Bradshaw of DSW? That'd be Kelly Cook. She loves fashion, she's obsessed with shoes (this is only a fraction of her collection— seriously, the woman has close to 400 pairs!), and she earned her nickname of "Runway Roadkill" after a very Carrie moment (read on to get all the details!). She's beyond honored to be the DSW spokesperson for this book, that'll soon become your new BFF.

Do You Speak Shoe Lover? sparked from her idea, *just a thought*, that there are SO MANY Shoe Lovers out there with stories to tell. Hilarious, romantic, endearing, captivating, uplifting stories (we're insanely grateful to everyone who shared theirs, by the way). And really, who wouldn't want to hear them—to be a part of the fabulousness of it all? The bond of shoe love is a powerful thing and this book is living proof. So thank you for purchasing, thank you for reading, and thank you for being a Shoe Lover.

QUESTIONS? COMMENTS?

Just want to dish about beautiful shoes?

REACH OUT TO KELLY AND THE TEAM OF DEDICATED SHOE LOVERS AT
DOYOUSPEAKSHOELOVER@DSWINC.COM.

CONTENTS

PART TWO   *TAKE IT FROM A SHOE LOVER*
Styling tips and savvy advice from the experts at DSW

PART THREE   *THE MAGIC BEHIND THE CURTAIN*
Why there's no place like DSW

FOREWORD

I've always loved shoes, and knew my whole life that shoe love was not just my passion alone. I spent the first few years of my professional life surrounding myself with fellow Shoe Lovers. Our shared obsession with this product prompted us to open a shoe store in 1969. We strongly believed that if we delivered great brands at great prices, the customers would come.

In those early years, we traveled around the world finding designers with high quality shoes, buying excess inventory wherever we could find it in order to deliver better brands to our customers. We knew Shoe Lovers would respond—and did they ever.

The building excitement for what we offered compelled us to rename our venture Designer Shoe Warehouse. It seemed like an obvious choice, as the store's underlying philosophy and the brand vision is to deliver designer shoes at warehouse prices.

I have to admit, traveling and finding great deals from amazing brands is one of the best parts about this business. For example, we were in Zurich when I fell in love with Bally shoes. We bought over 500,000 pairs to sell at a discount to our customers at DSW. I will always remember that day, because it was one of the times I knew our customers would love those shoes as much as I did.

We initially launched DSW in Ohio before making any significant geographic leap. We built a base in our hometown before expanding throughout the Midwest and Northeast. We positioned DSW as a discount retailer, reflecting our signature trait: providing great value to our customers.

As DSW gradually developed into a chain, our white and black striped color theme—most visible on the awnings in front of the company's stores—became a familiar sight in many markets. However, it is our love and passion for shoes that continues to earn the loyalty of the customers we serve: our Shoe Lovers.

I love being in a DSW store and watching the joy shoes bring our customers. From one Shoe Lover to another—enjoy the following pages, dedicated to Shoe Lovers everywhere!

Jay Schottenstein

Jay Schottenstein,
Shoe Lover & Chairman, DSW

DO SHOES PLAY A CRITICAL ROLE IN YOUR LIFE?

What we wear on our feet can affect our mood in a way that almost nothing else does. There's nothing quite like slipping on a brand new pair of shoes; it does something that the right jeans, dress, or a haircut just cannot. Finding the perfect shoe is a quick and easy fix for whatever is ailing you. No matter how bad your day is going—whether you need to lose five pounds, haven't blow-dried your hair, or put on a bit of makeup—none of this seems to matter if you have the perfect shoes. They can make you forget just about everything else and focus, even for a brief moment, on how good your feet look.

The two words at the center of our business—Shoe Lover—describe DSW's customers and employees. DSW has acknowledged that it is OK to be a Shoe Lover each and every season! This book is not about the psychology of a Shoe Lover; instead, it's a celebration of all things shoe love. It will embrace the Shoe Lover inside all of us, telling stories from fellow Shoe Lovers that will make you laugh, cry, or cringe, perhaps recognizing a little of yourself in them.

We will also give you practical tips from the always-stylish experts at DSW, to help you pick just the right shoe for every occasion in your life. From that important job interview to your wedding day and all those events in between, they will help guide you to the perfect shoe. The stylish experts at DSW (all self-proclaimed Shoe Lovers; you can't work there unless you are!) know how to provide the trends of the season at an irresistible value for all Shoe Lovers. They will take that talent and let us peek behind the curtain. Some will also share their own funny fashion emergencies—those rare moments that make us all cringe in recognition, since we all have them, don't we?

And this book won't just make all of us feel better about loving shoes—it will also tell us a little bit about the the brand that's striving to become America's Favorite Place for Shoes. They know that this is an impossible goal to achieve without the help of the 11,000 Shoe Lovers employed across the country. DSW is aware of the bit of wisdom that every successful business embraces: our associates are what make the true difference. If you care deeply about your employees, they will care just as deeply about your customers.

DSW's Shoe Lover values percolate from their headquarters in Columbus, Ohio, into each of their retail locations (375 and climbing), website (dsw.com), their over 21 million Rewards members, and over 2 million fans on Facebook.

In short, the DSW customer is loyal and obsessed with shoes!

1

SHOE LOVE
CHANGED MY LIFE

PERSONAL ACCOUNTS FROM THE
DSW FASHION-CRAZED FAITHFUL

SHOE STYLING
101

*Offset the toughness of these
ah-mazing studded flats with
something ultra feminine—
think full skirts or floral dresses.*

Miu Miu *Metallic Leather Studded Flat*

1

I MIGHT HAVE A PROBLEM

STORIES OF EPIC SHOE LOVE

"I was getting married on Valentine's Day, so of course I had to have the perfect red shoe for my special day. I found them; they were absolutely THE SHOE, red satin heels with bows on the back. They only had a size 8 left, I squeezed my size 9½ feet into them, figuring I only had to wear them for the ceremony then I'd take them off. They looked awesome. I couldn't feel my toes all night, but it was worth it!"

–Colleen Collins, Shoe Lover & Customer, Warwick, RI

Shoes equal love and emotion for many people and to buy someone shoes as a gift, or find that perfect shoe a friend has been hunting down all over town, is a way to show how much you love them! It's probably pretty clear by this point that we are writing this book because we are self-proclaimed Shoe Lovers. We just LOVE all kinds of shoes and know that this feeling is universal. In fact, according to Marshal Cohen, Fashion Industry Expert at NPD Group, women in the US are the number one shoe addicts in the world, buying an average of seven to eight new pairs a year.

HOW FAR WOULD YOU GO
TO SAVE THE FAMILY BUSINESS?

Kinky
Boots

"CHARLIE, I'D LIKE TO SHOW YOU THE MOST BEAUTIFUL THING IN THE WORLD. A LOT OF PEOPLE WOULD SAY...IT'S AN OAK TREE IN THE SPRING. OTHERS MIGHT SAY...IT'S A FIELD OF BEAUTIFUL FLOWERS. YOU KNOW WHAT I THINK IT IS, CHARLIE? IT'S. A. SHOE."

From *Kinky Boots*. Words of wisdom from Charlie's father before leaving him the family shoe business.

SO HOW DOES A SHOE LOVER COME TO BE?

Well, some certainly aren't born that way. Over time, they are exposed to people or situations that teach them to love shoes. Each and every shoe purchase in our closet builds on our love and obsession for shoes!

Sean Davis, a DSW Associate Content Management Specialist, thought he loved shoes before coming to work at DSW. He had no idea! Since working at DSW he has doubled the number of shoes he owns and gets dressed everyday starting with his shoes. His experience managing style content for dsw.com has helped him realize how important it is to have your own defined personal style.

At some point between the time we learned about the embarrassing riches of Imelda Marcos (the former first lady of the Philippines, who owned thousands of pairs of shoes), and our first meeting with Carrie Bradshaw, the Shoe Lover in all of us finally felt free to come out of the closet.

And did she ever! Carrie Bradshaw, Sarah Jessica Parker's character on *Sex and the City*, became synonymous with her extravagant obsession for shoes. Living in a small one-bedroom walkup in Manhattan, she notoriously and proudly spent all of her hard-earned money on ridiculously expensive shoes. Now there's a Shoe Lover to cheer for! Unlike Imelda, Carrie was completely self-made, self-supporting (if barely), and completely obsessed with shoes. *Sex and the City*, which captured the zeitgeist of the modern-day single woman, originally ran from 1998–2004. There were ninety-four episodes in all, many of which were dedicated to Carrie's shoe obsession.

66 *I have this little substance abuse problem:*
expensive footwear. 99

– Carrie Bradshaw

Carrie wasn't ashamed in the least bit that she spent all her money on clothes and shoes. In fact, one of her best lines from the series still has to be: *"I like my money where I can see it, hanging in my closet."* It wasn't until she was a little bit older (and perhaps a little wiser) that Carrie found herself broke, realizing: *"I've spent $40,000 on shoes and I have no place to live? I will literally be the old woman who lived in her shoes!"* This is one of the most memorable quotes that Carrie uttered—something she was forced to tell her friends when she found herself too broke to buy her apartment when it was going co-op. Carrie's character allowed the Shoe Lover in all of us to come out into the open. There is a Carrie in all of us—and we no longer have to feel embarrassed to be a Shoe Lover.

SHOES ARE AN EASY WAY TO TREAT OURSELVES

Although most of us don't have the disposable income (or have a little more sense) to spend more than our yearly rent on shoes, there is a universal love we feel for Carrie and fellow Shoe Lovers. Most Shoe Lovers hold a place in their heart for the first shoes they were able to buy for themselves—whether they were a pair of sneakers in grammar school or the expensive designer shoes they saved up for, they each trigger a "coming of age" memory they will always savor.

> "*I will never forget the first time my mom trusted me to pick out my own back-to-school clothes. I was in eighth grade and she gave me the money and told me to pick out my new wardrobe for school. I came home with 2 shirts, 1 pair of jeans, and 6 pairs of shoes!*"
>
> –Keyaush Dupree, Shoe Lover & Customer, Compton, CA

There are more blogs, Pinterest pages, and Facebook pages dedicated to shoe love than any other piece of women's clothing these days. Even sales of handbags, which have an obsessive quality all their own, can't hold a candle to the billions in shoe sales yearly in the US.

*"**I** hide my shoes from my neighbors. I keep them in my trunk and only bring them in the house at night. I had to after my neighbors kept asking, 'Don't you ever buy groceries? We only see you with DSW shopping bags!'"*

—Pat O'Connor, Shoe Lover & Store Manager, DSW

Shoes are an easy way to treat ourselves. No matter what kind of day you are having, a shoe will turn it around. Even if just for a short time, buying that new pair of platforms, fun Chuck Taylors, or splurging on a beautiful pair of Gucci pumps will make you feel instantly like new.

*"**M**y daughter heard about these 'Glass Slipper' shoes, and wanted them badly for her prom. We looked everywhere, even eBay, for her size. I finally went into our local DSW and to my delight, they had them! Better yet, they were on sale and we had a Rewards certificate. They ended up costing next to nothing. Thank you, DSW!"*

—Shari Nordstrom, Shoe Lover & Customer, Chicago, IL

Women represent the vast majority of the footwear business. They tend to buy not just for themselves, but their entire family. For most people, buying shoes all year round for an entire family only seems to feed the obsession.

LOVE IS GRAND

SHOE
LOVE

DSW
MOTTO

IS EPIC

> *"The emotional attachment people—especially women—have with shoes is absolutely fantastic! From the minute you walk into DSW our main goal is to make you love us and our shoes!"*

—Jim O'Donnell, Shoe Lover & Board of Directors Member, DSW

ACCORDING TO *HARPER'S BAZAAR* MAGAZINE, ONE IN TWO WOMEN OWNS MORE THAN 30 PAIRS OF SHOES. THAT'S DEFINITELY OUR KIND OF WOMAN!

Even famed pop artist Andy Warhol was a Shoe Lover. He created print after print of shoes: some illustrations, some with booties, all breathtaking masterpieces featuring shoes as his muse.

So how do you know if your shoe love is a shoe obsession? And is that a bad thing? We embrace all that makes a person a Shoe Lover and help you feed that obsession at every price point!

> ## "America has a love affair with shoes, which we're happy to be a part of!"
>
> —Jay Schottenstein, Shoe Lover & Chairman, DSW

DSW offers shoes at every price point available, with enough different styles to whet the appetite of even the most shoe obsessed Shoe Lover.

Yes—we may occasionally make impulsive shoe choices that maybe we shouldn't have. Admit it—we have all been there! We've purchased a pair we thought would be perfect—then got them home and realized that not only do they not go with anything in our closet; they also are a size too small! And then there are the times we were so excited that we wore them all day, in the rain—so there's no looking back now. At times like these, we can hide them in our closets and try to forget about them. Or, we can try to make them work. If they really don't fit or don't work in with your lifestyle, well that's what eBay is for, right?

*"**I** am such a Shoe Lover that I would rather shop for shoes at DSW than go out for lunch!"*

—Leonora Uribe, Shoe Lover & Customer, Plantation, FL

*"**I** buy a lot of shoes! I have so many that when I started running out of room in my closet and my daughter went to college, I took over her bedroom—first just a corner, then the entire room— and made it my 'adjunct' shoe closet. My daughter was so upset when she came home for the summer that I had to donate about half my shoes to a charity of her choice to calm her down. Despite her accusations, I really don't love my shoes more than her!"*

—Constance Pandolfo, Shoe Lover & Customer, Hatfield, PA

*"**I** am such a shoe addict! I actually leave the five or so pairs that I buy at a time in the trunk of my car. Then I bring them in the house, one pair at a time over a couple of days. That way I don't feel so guilty and I turn each new pair into its own fun treat!"*

Alicia Peake, Shoe Lover & Women's Buyer for dsw.com, DSW

Men don't seem to have these problems. For most men, speaking Shoe Lover is like speaking a foreign language. Actress and writer Mindy Kaling shared a hilarious take on men and shoes in her book *Is Everyone Hanging Out Without Me: "I really think guys only need two pairs of shoes: a nice pair of black shoes and a pair of Chuck Taylors."* Men seem to have it so easy, don't they? Or do they just miss out on the fun? Some men don't think it's time to get a new pair of shoes until they can stand on a quarter and tell whether it's heads or tails!

Don't get us wrong; men can be Shoe Lovers, too. Even Forrest Gump's classic red, white, and blue Nike running shoes are iconic! And, of course, they were a gift from Jenny, his lifelong love.

However, for the most part, men do not want to work for it. They don't enjoy the hunt the way most women do. They want the shoe-buying process to be easy and straightforward. That's exactly one of the reasons why men like buying their shoes at DSW—easy to see the shoes, easy to find their size. Not only that, they can get their technical athletic shoes, their loafers, and their boots—all in the same place. Talk about efficient!

When men shop, they are much more results-oriented; that is, they're looking to buy, not to shop. While women enjoy the shopping experience as much as finding something to purchase, men are the opposite; they want to find what they're seeking as quickly as possible.

"THESE ARE MY NEW SHOES. THEY'RE GOOD SHOES. THEY WON'T MAKE YOU RICH LIKE ME, THEY WON'T MAKE YOU REBOUND LIKE ME, THEY DEFINITELY WON'T MAKE YOU HANDSOME LIKE ME. THEY'LL ONLY MAKE YOU HAVE SHOES LIKE ME, THAT'S IT." –CHARLES BARKLEY

"*When I met my wife, I would have been happy being either barefoot or in flip-flops every day of my life. From the time we were first dating, I knew she was obsessed with shoes; but it wasn't until our first Christmas together as husband and wife that she surprised me with two pairs of shoes—she started slowly. She knew exactly what to buy me to start my own shoe obsession. After that, I let her buy all my shoes for me. Over the years, she has stocked me with enough shoes that I never have to wear flip-flops again!*"

–Eric Brown, Shoe Lover & Customer, Plano, TX

NOW, NOT ALL SHOE LOVERS ARE PEOPLE.

DOGS HAPPEN TO ALSO LOVE SHOES,

ESPECIALLY PUPPIES.

This adorable pup belongs to one of our very own Shoe Lovers, and we're dying to send it in to dogshaming.com! (Don't you just love that site? It's brilliant!)

I ATE YOUR SHOES.

(SORRY I'M NOT SORRY.)

SHOE NOTES

(LIKE CLIFF'S, BUT WAY MORE FABULOUS!)

1

Billions of dollars worth of shoes are sold each year in the US. We're so pumped to be a big part of that fun!

2

Shoe love is all emotion. This is one of the reasons why we love coming to work every day. To see all of that happiness.

3

Lunch hour? Try shoe-shopping hour! DSW is a great place to go on your lunch break.

SHOE STYLING
101

*The black and gold trend is big
(BIG, big!) so don't be afraid
to wear these with every single
thing in your closet.*

Franco Sarto *Elfie Talula Boot*

2
WHAT I DID FOR SHOE LOVE
SHAMELESS ACTS OF FOOTWEAR FANATICS

"*I was living in Southern California a few years ago when the wildfires were happening across the area. It got so bad that our neighborhood was forced to evacuate. And what was the very first thing I did when we got the news? I grabbed my 20 most favorite pairs of shoes to take with me! Not my wedding pictures, not my baby's keepsakes—but my shoes. And it was hard, too, having to leave behind all my other gorgeous pairs. Thankfully, everything was fine and we were able to return home. I'd never get over it if ALL my shoes were gone forever! (My photos and baby's stuff, too!)*"

Andre Harris, Shoe Lover & Customer, Houston, TX

Everyone has a shoe memory that involves some facet of shoe regret—a pair they didn't buy, one they misplaced or gave away—just something they can't seem to get out of their mind.

"A friend of my daughter needed a fabulous pair of strappy sandals for an event. I lent her an entire suitcase—twelve pairs of the most gorgeous, blingy, sparkly shoes I owned—from which to choose. When she returned them somehow my daughter mixed them up with things in the garage to give away—and wouldn't you know it? My husband threw the entire suitcase away! It took me a month to realize it, and by then they were long gone. Now each and every time I have an event to go to, I get sad and then angry all over again thinking about my long lost pairs of shoes!"

Colleen Marshall, Shoe Lover & Co-Anchor, NBC4, Columbus, OH

Then there are those they just had to have and bought after overcoming obstacles— whether they could not afford them, did not really "need" them, or were kept from them.

" I am 53 now, but I will never forget what my mother and I did to get me a pair of patent leather Buster Brown shoes when I was ten years old. Not only could we not really afford them; it also took forever for us to find them. When I finally got them, I felt like a real live princess whenever I wore them. I will always be grateful to my parents for making me feel so special with those shoes."

–Deb Ramirez, Shoe Lover & Customer, Lansing, MI

" I had to have these black pumps in my closet. They were, of course, way too expensive for me—but I didn't care. As I went up to the register to pay for them I figured out how many nights I'd have to eat Frosted Flakes for dinner to pay for them!"

–Ashley Simmons, Shoe Lover & Assistant Buyer, DSW

A major aspect of what makes a person a real Shoe Lover is their ability to become so obsessed with a particular shoe they just have to buy. Some people actually say they hear a shoe singing their name on the shelf or in a magazine. The ends that they will go to justify, convince, split across however many payments, credit cards, or pay-later plans to make it happen can be extreme to an outside observer—but not to a fellow Shoe Lover! Heck, some of us save the shopping bags and boxes to remember our special shoe purchases. Even Penny (a character, played by Kaley Cuoco) on the CBS TV series *The Big Bang Theory* has a DSW bag in her closet to show off that shoe love.

THE ENDS THAT SHOE LOVERS WILL GO TO CAN BE EXTREME TO AN OUTSIDE OBSERVER— BUT NOT TO A FELLOW SHOE LOVER!

There are certainly times when you have to talk yourself into buying a pair of shoes. You work hard to somehow convince yourself they are a staple and you must own them! You start stalking them in stores and online—you can't get them out of your head. And then when you finally cave and go to buy them, it's too late. They're sold out everywhere in your size and that makes you want them even more! It becomes your mission. You spend days, weeks, even years browsing different sites and shopping clearance sales. Finally, you come to terms with the fact that they've officially become "the shoes that got away."

For some people, it's as much about the thrill of the chase as the actual purchase.

FOR US? IT'S THIS AMAZING PAIR VERSACE PLATFORMS. THEY ARE ABSOLUTELY THE ONES THAT TOTALLY GOT AWAY. SO IF ANYONE, ANYONE (YES, WE'RE BEGGING HERE, SHOE LOVERS!) HAS A PAIR THEY'RE WILLING TO PART WITH, DROP US A LINE AT DOYOUSPEAKSHOELOVER@DSWINC.COM. WE'LL HAPPILY TAKE THEM OFF YOUR HANDS!

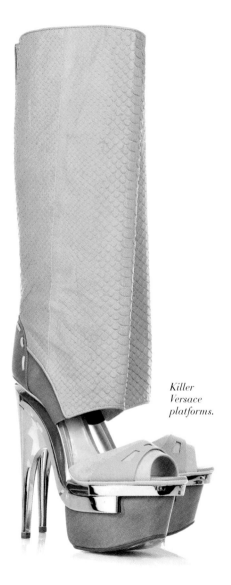

Killer Versace platforms.

You may even dream about them at night. Sometimes the hunt for them is just as satisfying as owning the actual pair of shoes!

> *"I had been dreaming about owning a pair of Christian Louboutins for much of my adult life. I knew it wasn't a realistic goal given my budget; but those red bottoms were calling out to me! My mom knew my dream—so she bought me a pair for a wedding one year. It was simply the best day of my life. I snuck them in my room when my husband wasn't looking. When he asked me about them, I said, 'Oh these old things? I've had them forever.' But then he saw the red bottoms one night at dinner, and he just about had a heart attack. Even he knew what that meant!"*
>
> –Daniella Bonfante, Shoe Lover & Merchandise Support Assistant, DSW

THOSE RED BOTTOMS WERE CALLING OUT TO ME!

Some shoes, like Louboutins, have reached such high levels of cult status, that it is more about owning and being seen wearing those red bottom soles than the shoes themselves. They have become status symbols in and of themselves and owning a pair makes you part of an exclusive club.

A Shoe Lover's well-loved (and well-worn!) Louboutins.

Then there are the shoes that seem to come through for you right when you need them.

"*I was absolutely dying for the coolest color soccer shoes. They didn't have them in my size anywhere so I bought one size bigger. I thought that if I wore an extra pair of thick socks I'd be okay. The day of the big game came, someone kicked the ball my way, I kicked it forward as hard as I could, and sent my shoe flying along with the ball into the goal. The goalie caught my shoe and missed the ball—and we won the game!*"

Catherine Willis, Shoe Lover & Customer, Troy, MI

Or maybe the ones you "borrowed" from a friend that you never returned.

"*Back when I played baseball for the Atlanta Braves, we only had one or two pairs of cleats each (we had to buy them ourselves). My pair was still wet from the game the day before, so I borrowed Joe Pepitone's cleats. I still remember everything about them; they were black with white stripes, and the leather was all broken in and comfortable. I told him, 'you're on the bench, so I'm wearing your shoes.' I hit two homeruns that night! Afterwards, Joe said to me, 'those cleats never did that for me!' I kept them and told him they were my lucky cleats now!*"

—Hank Aaron, Shoe Lover,
Baseball Hall of Fame inductee 1982,
& Board of Directors Member, DSW

AND OF COURSE, THERE ARE THE LENGTHS THAT PEOPLE WILL GO TO WEAR OR PROTECT THEIR FAVORITE PAIR OF SHOES.

"*I will never forget the fight I got into with my best friend over a pair of shoes. They weren't just any shoes; they were my favorite heels at the time. I had just bought them and was so excited to wear them out on a big Friday night. My car broke down in the pouring rain. We had to get out and try to push the car out of a huge puddle. She got out and started pushing—but I didn't join her. She started to get angry at me and asked what the heck I thought I was doing. I protested: 'but my shoes!' I finally wrapped my shoes in my sweatshirt and got out of the car barefoot to help. I know my friend was mad at me—but all I cared about was saving those shoes!*"

Armina Iapichino, Shoe Lover & Customer, San Antonio, TX

THE WIZARD OF OZ

TWO GIRLS. ONE FABULOUS PAIR OF HEELS.
SOMEONE'S NOT MAKING IT OUT ALIVE.

"*I* have always loved high-heeled mules, but for some reason they don't love me back! I was attending a very fancy, very fabulous award dinner in New York. On the dance floor I literally lost my right shoe, it slipped right

---

Carolee Friedlander, Shoe Lover & Board of Directors Member, DSW

---

off my foot! That's not the first time I have lost a mule, I was running across 5th Avenue in Manhattan, trying to make the light before it turned red and the same shoe slipped right off my foot. What we do in the name of fashion!"

"I was going out with girlfriends from college, and had on gorgeous killer stiletto boots. One of my heels broke as we were walking into a club. I didn't want to ruin the night, so I broke the other heel off and stayed out all night. You only would have noticed if you saw me up close—but at the club in the dark, I looked great!"

–Ashley Simmons, Shoe Lover & Assistant Buyer, DSW

"I sprained my ankle, so I can't really wear my killer heels to work. But I sneak them every once in a while, taking off my brace and putting on a medium heel so I feel great at work. And the best part—my physical therapist gave me the okay, since she's a Shoe Lover too!"

–Tammy Culpepper, Shoe Lover & Sales Associate, DSW

"I was getting out of a taxi and I somehow got my coat stuck in the door. As the taxi driver began to pull away, I wasn't thinking 'oh—this could be really bad or I could possibly be maimed or killed!' Instead I was thinking, 'Oh no, I'm going to ruin my shoes if he drives off and I have to run along side his car until I get my coat loose.'"

–Eva Schmatz, Shoe Lover & Customer, New York, NY

THE HUNT FOR THE PERFECT SHOE MAY SOMETIMES BECOME OBSESSIVE, BUT IT ALWAYS PRODUCES HAPPINESS IN THE END.

"I saw this amazing pair of shoes from men's shoe designer Oliver Sweeney in a magazine, and I knew I had to have them! I finally tracked them down and bought them—and they are now displayed in my closet like a piece of art. I have never actually worn them, but they make me so happy every time I look at them. I love owning them."

—Harris Mustafa, Shoe Lover
& EVP Supply Chain Planning
& Allocation, DSW

We all know that a shameless act of shoe love can also downplay the price and turn you into the sneakiest of shoppers. We actually know women that keep red pens in their closet so that they can mark through the price on the shoebox when they get home. That way, if their spouse happens to ask them about their new shoes, they can quickly show them the box and say, "Yeah, but I got them on sale! See the red line?"

How many times have we all bought a pair of shoes in the wrong size or they were just plain uncomfortable? But we justify that purchase in our minds somehow; they may not fit us now but they'll fit us later; my feet are swollen; I'm retaining water; they'll work next season; I have the wrong socks on—the list can go on and on.

"*My shoe obsession started at a very young age. My family had very little while I was growing up. With two older sisters and no money, all my shoes were well worn—many with holes in them—before I got the next pair. When I was 14 years old, I got my first real job taking on a paper route. I immediately saved my money; my first purchase was a brand new pair of Bass Moccasins. I remember them like it was yesterday!*"

–Jim Robbins, Shoe Lover & Former Board of Directors Member, DSW

SHOE NOTES

(LIKE CLIFF'S, BUT WAY MORE FABULOUS!)

1

The one that got away. Yikes.
At our irresistible values—everyday—you never have to
worry about the one that got away!

2

Just like Hank, sometimes we hit a home run by borrowing
a pair from a friend.

3

The hunt.
Boy—that's one of the best parts of shopping at DSW!

A pair of shoes can change your life— just ask Cinderella

SHOE STYLING
—— 101 ——

Saving this beauty just for big events?
Don't! Jeans and your favorite tee
will play down glamour.

The Glass Slipper Collection *Cinderella Pump*

3

FEET, DON'T FAIL ME NOW!

HOW SHOES GET US THROUGH LIFE'S BIG MOMENTS

"I knew my wife was waiting for the Disney/DSW Glass Slipper Collection to be released, because she talked about it all the time. I hadn't seen her this excited since…well, ever! So I decided the perfect place to ask her to marry me would be at DSW, when the shoe came into the store. I worked everything out with the incredibly helpful store manager beforehand. I hid in the back of the store while my wife looked for her size. When she couldn't find it, the manager walked over to help. My palms were getting sweaty as I clutched the box in the back room, waiting for the manager to alert me over the walkie-talkie when I should make my entrance. My heart was practically beating out of my chest by the time I heard my wife's voice. I peeked out and saw her waiting, and slowly walked towards her, carrying the box with the ring planted in the shoe. She was so surprised to see me carrying the box she didn't know what to expect. I got down on one knee and everyone in the store gathered around us. She opened the box and screamed as she saw the ring box inside. She was so excited and in such shock that she didn't know what to do or say! Once she calmed down I asked her; she said yes, and the entire store broke out into applause. Needless to say, those are definitely her favorite pair of shoes now.

— Mike Keane, Shoe Lover & Customer, Lubbock, TX

SHOES CAN MAKE A BAD DAY GOOD

The perfect killer heel can change your mood almost instantly. Unlike your weight, hair, skin, or anything else involved with your looks that isn't so easily altered, shoes can give an easy lift to your day. And even if nothing else does, shoes always fit. As Los Angeles–based Customer & Shoe Lover Brinley Turner explains, *"No other piece of clothing (not your jeans, a top, or a jacket) can possibly prompt a compliment much like a pair of shoes. No one ever asks, 'how do these jeans look on me' unless they want to brace themselves for something they may not want to hear, right? But shoes never make you worry that you look fat, have a muffin top, or a big rear end. They just always fit."*

Simply put, shoes equal happiness. Even Dorothy had to click her beautiful ruby red slippers together to get home! Shoes can become part of your family or feel like a best friend, adopting their own personality and identity in your closet.

According to DSW President & CEO Mike MacDonald, "When we opened our State Street store in Chicago, I got to meet some amazing customers. One customer had over 350 pairs of shoes and was so proud of the system in which she organized them. I'll never forget her. She actually called her shoes her friends."

We see it every day at DSW: a customer walks into the store. They may be worried about something. They may be in a funk. They may just need a break from an otherwise crazy day, or want to buy something fabulous to make them feel better. Let's face it; some days we feel great. But other days, we feel like a busted can of biscuits. And that's OK—because shopping for shoes can cure it all! In fact, one DSW customer told us that all she needed in order to conquer the world was "pumps, pantyhose, and pearls!"

"When I feel bad I like to treat myself. Clothes never look any good…food just makes me fatter…shoes always fit." – *In Her Shoes*, 2005

A customer will wander up and down the aisles—sometimes with a goal in mind, sometimes not. She makes her way toward a shoe on display, hesitates, and picks it up to inspect it more closely. She sits down and slips it on. "Wow," a smile breaks out on her face. "What a difference a shoe makes," she thinks as she gingerly removes the other shoe from the box, slips it on, and teeters towards a mirror where an even bigger smile emerges. She has just experienced shoe love!

*Not only do shoes make you feel great, **they each have a story to tell.** Isn't it a great feeling walking through your closet—picking up each shoe and remembering what you were doing, where you were strutting, how you were creating that amazing life moment? **It all happened in THAT shoe.***

"When I was leaving to go abroad to college in Turin, Italy, my mom and I went shopping for the perfect shoe to take with me. I wanted to look hip and stylish in Italy. We knew it would be cold and my mom was insistent that I take as few pairs of shoes as possible. I bought a pair of black and white furry snow boots that I loved and wore the entire semester. They kept me warm, and reminded me of my mom and of home when I was feeling lonely. And I looked totally cool and felt like a hip European. To this day when I see pictures of myself from that trip, those boots make me smile and remind me what it was like to be young and adventurous."

– Divya Allupeddinti, Shoe Lover & Customer, Tempe, AZ

SHOES ARE LIFE'S LITTLE NARRATORS— ALL WITH A **STORY TO TELL**

Another pair of Jim's favorite shoes— combat boots he's worn for decades!

SHOES
MAKE A STATEMENT.

Yes, often about fashion, but also one of encouragement and love. When NFL players decided to show their support for the Susan B. Komen Breast Cancer Foundation in recent years, they did it by wearing bright pink cleats during their games. Without having to say a word, they used their shoes to tell a very important story, and express their encouragement for this incredibly important cause.

"After my divorce I decided to start over—I mean with everything! Because I was moving as well, I gave away almost all my things except my shoes—all 150 pairs. It wasn't easy transporting all of them to Florida from New York. The back 2 rows of my car were filled with shoes. But I just couldn't part with them; they all bring me such happiness, even at the darkest of times."

– Danielle Lopato, Shoe Lover & Customer, Bradenton, FL

"You sold your soul to the devil when you put on your first pair of Jimmy Choos, I saw it."

– The Devil Wears Prada, 2006

Our love and passion for a particular pair of shoes can even get us into trouble once in a while. As Shoe Lovers, we often make the best memories in our best shoes—even when they're memories we'd prefer to forget:

"I will always remember my 30th birthday. My husband threw me a surprise party at a piano bar. I was sitting on the edge of the piano when someone I didn't know took off my shoe, sang to me and then poured his beer in my shoe and drank from it! Yuck! Good thing they weren't my favorite pair; I could never wear them again!"

– Doye Williams, Shoe Lover & Customer, Wichita, KS

"I always loved shoes, and my husband knew it. On our honeymoon in Paris, we went to a famous French store called Galeries Lafayette and he bought me a pair of shoes as a wedding present. Now he buys me a pair of shoes on every vacation. They are my glorious and fabulous souvenirs."

Sarah Azevedo, Shoe Lover & Customer, Grand Rapids, MI

AND SOMETIMES SHOES ARE USED T MARK A SPECIAL EVENT OR DAY, AN BECOME A TRADITION

"My husband and I are on a fitness program which requires us to weigh in every week. He does it in the morning, and I do so after work. The last time I weighed in, a newer girl in the gym asked me where I work. When I told her, she said, 'Speaking of shoes, there's this hot guy who comes in every week to weigh in and we're always checking out his shoes. He's always got on great shoes!' I asked her if his name was Tim. She said 'Yes'—I started laughing. I told her that's my husband—and I buy his shoes at DSW! Hey—you gotta support the brand!"

Jo Ann Martin, Shoe Lover & Senior Director Merchandise Planning
& Item Planning, DSW

SHOE NOTES

(LIKE CLIFF'S, BUT WAY MORE FABULOUS!)

1

*Shoes can make a bad day good—we have
over 400 brands of shoes in stores and at dsw.com.
Can you say no more bad days?*

2

*Shoes tell a story. With 15,000 pairs in each store, we want
you to have lots and lots of stories in your closet.*

3

*Shoes are the new souvenirs. What great memories!
Pick up a fab pair on your next vacay.*

SHOE STYLING
101

Show off the sexiness of these strappy little numbers by keeping your legs bare. (People wanna see those details!)

KG by Kurt Geiger *Elfie Reptile Suede Sandal*

4

WHERE'D YOU GET THOSE SHOES?

BONDING OVER FABULOUS FASHION

Those five simple words, strung together like a musical prose, can bring people together. To many people, a shoe compliment is the highest form of praise one can get and give. Ask someone about their shoes, or throw out an "I love your shoes," and you will instantly get a warm response, a smile, or even a big old hug. It really is the best universal conversation starter.

> **"I** *love shoes. Even if I'm not buying them, I'm trying them on. And I seem to meet a fellow Shoe Lover everywhere I go. Telling someone, 'I love your shoes' is an instant icebreaker, wherever you are. I once found myself at the airport with a bag that was five pounds over the weight limit. When I unzipped it and the attendant saw that my fabulous shoe collection was weighing my bag down, she laughed—and didn't charge me extra. She must have been a fellow Shoe Lover!"*

Sharbreon Plummer, Shoe Lover & Customer, Metairie, LA

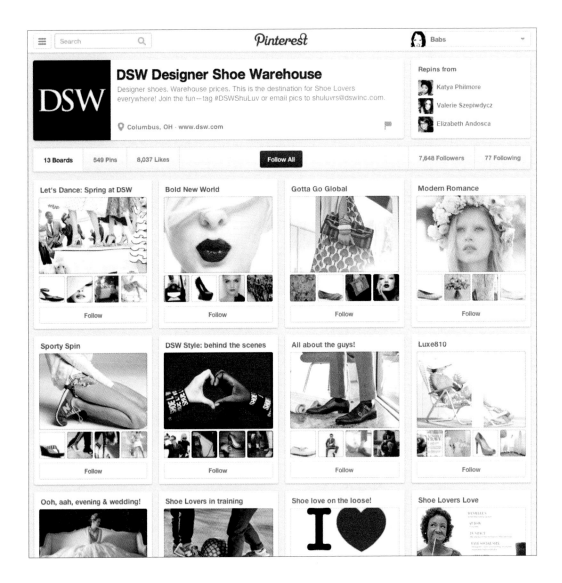

Shoes bring people together; shoe love is universal. Everyone seems to be able to remember a story from their past about a particular pair of shoes—and there's usually a particular person attached to that shoe memory.

> *"My best friend lives in San Antonio, about five hours away from me. Our shoes bring us together; we take pictures and text them to each other daily. Since I rarely, if ever, repeat a shoe, she challenged me to see how long I could go before repeating the same shoe. It took me three months and a few days before I was finally done! I want her to challenge me again—because thanks to DSW, I have replenished my shoe collection!"*
>
> –Ashley Bruman, Shoe Lover & Customer, Plano, TX

The Internet is full of blog posts, Pinterest boards, Facebook pages, and Twitter feeds where people refer to their love of shoes. They dedicate countless posts and photos, writing paragraph after paragraph describing their love for a particular pair of shoes. Some are even romantic, writing haikus and poetry to their favorite pair. A recent Internet search for shoes produced over 807 million websites and almost 2 million blogs. That's a whole lot of shoe love!

"*I have so many pairs of shoes (thanks to DSW) that in order to curb the addiction, I decided to make a New Year's resolution to not purchase any new shoes until I have worn each and every pair in my closet. I am even blogging about my experience.*"

–Kristen Becker, Shoe Lover & Customer, Wharton, NJ

PEOPLE OFTEN ASSOCIATE THEIR SHOES WITH HELPING THEM GET OVER AN EMOTIONAL OR TOUGH TIME IN THEIR LIVES, JUST AS A FRIEND WOULD.

"*When I first moved with my family to Ohio, we didn't know anyone. Our very first Sunday morning we all went to this little restaurant nearby called Early Birds Breakfast. The owner, Sarah, asked us what brought us to Ohio, and I told her we moved for my new job at DSW. Everyone went crazy! They rang this big cowbell on the wall announcing to everyone that a Shoe Lover was in the house! They were so welcoming that it's become our family ritual to eat breakfast at Early Birds EVERY Sunday, no matter what.*"

–Kelly Cook, Shoe Lover & SVP Marketing, DSW

ODE TO THE SHOE

Oh, stilletto heels
You make my feet ache dancing
But I love you so
Rushing through the rain
In my brand new riding boots
Avoid the puddles, please
It's casual Friday
But these lacey, glitter pumps
Are all business
Peep-toe and patent
This is the start of a
Shoe love story

Written by Alyssa Eckles,
Shoe Lover & Customer, Cleveland, OH

Bonding over shoe love is as easy between friends as it is between mothers and daughters. However, it doesn't always go according to plan.

A customer shared this photo on Facebook with a funny story: Her daughter was so excited to show her mom her sequin stilettos from DSW that she forgot she had neglected to tell her mom about her crown tattoo on the top of her foot—which is clearly visible in the photo. Oops!

Shoe love can sometimes be done incognito. At a recent Shoe Struck event in a New Jersey DSW store, a lucky young customer told us, *"I am over-the-moon excited about being Shoe Struck—but please, don't put my picture on DSW's Facebook page. I called in sick to work today to be here!"*

SHOE LOVERS FOR LIFE!

JUST A FEW OF OUR FAVE PICS FROM THE DSW FACEBOOK PAGE.

This lucky lady won an all-expense-paid trip to Disney just for styling the gorgeous Glass Slipper Collection shoes!

2011's most popular DSW Facebook photo. (Chic babies rule!)

Gorgeous wedge sandals go everywhere—
EVERYWHERE. And this Shoe Lover totally proves it.

Your shoe collection: thrown in a box
or displayed proudly on shelves?
Facebook Shoe Lovers were totally split!

Guy loves girl. **Girl loves shoes.**

We're always up for a round of flats
(**especially** the Steve Madden Heaven)!

Hint, hint: love is best
expressed with **highly-
addictive contents** boxes.

Audrey Brooke suede pumps
+ mad styling skills
= one crazy-hot outfit!

Rewards certificates and Facebook Frenzy surprises paid for these sweet little kicks!

Not sure what's cooler: the movie-star-fabulous heels or the shut-the-front-door price (just $49⁹⁵)!

You're never too young to rock a pair of Converse sneakers!

News flash: leopard is a neutral. This Shoe Lover paired her Fergalicious pumps with a bright and bold dress. Makes you smile, doesn't it?

Seasonless boots? You love them. We love them. The whole entire world loves them.

Now that's a statement bag— Shoe Lovers represent!

Kids' shoes on dsw.com? We made it happen. And we asked our Facebook Shoe Lovers to pick out their fave pair for this little looker!

Fergalicious shoes are just so, so good, aren't they? We had a contest to see how our Shoe Lovers would style 'em and this look completely won us over.

One Shoe Lover's Christmas gifts! (She must've been good—**really** good!)

This dress? That bag? Amazing, right? Here's the winning look from our handbag styling contest!

Shoe love is true love, people.

SHOE NOTES

(LIKE CLIFF'S, BUT WAY MORE FABULOUS!)

1

*DSW. It's where you get those shoes. And handbags.
And scarves. And belts. And clutches. And iPad cases.
And wallets. And kids' shoes.*

2

*807 million websites mention "shoes."
We're thrilled to be a part of all that shoe love!*

3

*You never know what will happen to you
at a DSW. Shoe Struck, anyone?*

SHOE STYLING
101

*Denim and dresses, meet
your match. This cooler-than-cool
platform bootie is a keeper
year-round.*

Modern Vintage *Jenie Bootie*

5

THANKS FOR THE MEMORIES

NOSTALGIC STORIES OF SHOE LOVE

"I moved to the 'big city' a few years ago, leaving my family, friends, and boyfriend behind. I can't get home more than once a year—but when I do, my mom, sisters, and I have a tradition. As soon as I get off the plane, we drive directly to our favorite DSW and shop 'til we drop. No matter how far away I live or how much we have all changed (especially my style), we can still bond over shoes! Last year I landed on Christmas Eve, and laughed and shopped until closing time!"

Chloe West, Shoe Lover & Customer, Chantilly, VA

MAYBE IT'S JUST A MEMORY OF A CERTAIN PLACE OR TIME IN OUR LIFE THAT A CERTAIN SHOE CAN SPARK. FROM THE SHOE WE WORE TO OUR FIRST HIGH SCHOOL DANCE TO THE FIRST DAY ON THE JOB, *SHOES MAKE US REMEMBER*, SMILE (OR CRINGE) AS WE RECALL THAT TIME.

"*I was starting the coolest new job ever—writing for my favorite TV show. It was truly my dream job! I was visiting the set in North Carolina for filming and just had to buy a fabulous pair of shoes for the occasion. I literally spent almost half my paycheck on these shoes. The day I arrived on the set, everyone—from the lead actresses to the members of the crew—were complimenting me on how 'cool' my shoes were. I was smiling ear-to-ear—that is, until I jumped out of the director's chair and landed on a bad ankle— and broke my foot! When I arrived to the set on crutches the next day, everyone cheered for me. I figured they'd always remember the girl who broke her foot in the name of fashion!*"

–Hadley Davis, Shoe Lover & Customer, Los Angeles, CA

"*I was the store manager of a Nine West at a mall in Ohio. I needed to reset the displays in the front window and as usual, I was wearing gorgeous, strappy sky-high sandals. As I carefully squeezed between the windows and the displays, I noticed a couple of good-looking guys staring at me through the window. Knowing I had an audience, I shimmied between and began putting the shoes on the glass blocks supported by cinder blocks—which, unfortunately, began to fall. Because I wasn't about to let a cinder block hit my shoe, I let it hit my toe instead. Ouch! It hurt so bad! I turned around and the hot guy was laughing at me, saying: 'We can't believe you let that fall on your toe instead of just letting it hit your shoes!' All I could say was… you just don't get it!*"

–Ifey Chukwumah, Shoe Lover & Customer, Columbus, OH

JUST ABOUT EVERY MEMORY CAN REMIND A TRUE SHOE LOVER OF A CERTAIN PAIR OF SHOES.

A shoe can conjure up memories of everything from the good (marriage proposals), the bad (breakups), and everything in between (first day of high school). Some stories don't even require us to say anything more than "those red shoes" to remind us of all the juicy details that we want to remember—and maybe some we don't!

"

"My family moved when I was in junior high, and I was about to start a new school. We went shopping and my mom let me pick out whatever shoes I wanted. I chose a pair of lace-ups with a great big heel and were two-toned yellow and brown. I felt like I was the coolest kid in town with them; I will never forget them!" —Kathy Stevens Ring, Shoe Lover & Customer, Salem, OR

For some people, shoes can elicit so much emotion and memories that they cannot be described with one word. In fact, we did an informal poll with some DSW Facebook Fans and around our office and found that on average people use twenty-seven words to describe their favorite shoes. That's a lot of detail for one pair of shoes!

How many times have you felt like a pair of shoes have spoken to you, calling out to you from their display? Some may have even sung to you. And even though you probably don't NEED them, you yearn for them in the same way you would for someone you love. They may even take on their own persona in your closet. For some Shoe Lovers, it can be a problem to attach a memory to each and every pair of shoes. How can you ever recycle a pair of shoes that you wore to prom? Your wedding? Your first day at the job you love? If every shoe reminds you of an event or time in your life, throwing them away is like tossing out memories!

SOMETIMES, THE MOST FANTASTIC MEMORIES ARE THE SIMPLEST ONES— EVEN WHEN THEY REQUIRE OUR IMAGINATION.

"*Everyone knows I love shoes—even my four-year-old grandson, who plays in my closet and goes shoe shopping with me. He gave me a pair of imaginary shoes for my birthday. I 'oohed and aahed' when he gave them to me. They are the best, most priceless shoes I have ever had!*"

—Kim Davis, Shoe Lover & Customer, Oakwood Village, OH

"*I love my shoes. I love the smell of a fresh pair of suede pumps, the feel of supple leather, and the sound heels make on the floor. I believe in serendipity and kismet; if a pair of shoes and I are meant to be together, they will somehow end up in my closet.*" —Nancy Szarkowski, Shoe Lover & Customer, Elkins Park, PA

"*I bought this killer pair of black patent leather, platform pumps because I knew Damon (my now husband) was going to propose to me. I wore them all night, through the appetizer (no proposal), the entrée (no proposal), and dessert (still no proposal!). They weren't exactly comfortable, so when we got home I slipped them off and threw on my dirty, sandy flip-flops from the beach. And wouldn't you know it—that was the exact moment he decided to get down on one knee and propose. I told him to wait a second and I put those black pumps back on my feet for my answer (which was yes!). I will never get rid of them!*" —Kelly Cook, Shoe Lover & SVP Marketing, DSW

SHOE NOTES

(LIKE CLIFF'S, BUT WAY MORE FABULOUS!)

1

First job interview shoes? DSW.
Wedding shoes? DSW.
Absolutely mind-blowing perfect birthday gift for your wife? DSW.

2

Shoe stories are epic—
we love hearing them all!

3

The smell, the feel, the sound. Shoes excite our senses.

SHOE STYLING
101

*Shake up your wardrobe
with high-top wedge sneakers.
They're totally edgy with
skinnies or leggings.*

Wanted *Gramercy Wedge Sneaker*

6

FUN, FLIRTY, AND FASHIONABLE

HOW DSW SATISFIES YOUR SHOE OBSESSION

> **❝ I never visit DSW without buying at least one pair of shoes. It is my job and my duty to support my company, or at least that's what I tell myself! ❞**
>
> Camille Merkle, Shoe Lover & Senior Manager Customer Engagement, DSW

DSW's "fun, flirty, and fashionable" take on shoes lets the Shoe Lover in everybody come out and play. You can literally hear screaming Shoe Lovers going crazy over the low prices on designer shoes from the clearance racks in the back of the stores. DSW has something for everyone. This makes it hard to resist buying shoes for every occasion, sometimes daily even. Part of shoe love includes sharing the news of shoes. Some of DSW's fans post "good morning" and "good night" on DSW's Facebook page. Every once in a while they'll post in the middle of the night about a shoe-tastic dream they had about a particular pair of shoes.

And of course, they shop—sometimes on a daily basis. They also gush about their shoes to their family, friends, and work colleagues—really, anyone who will listen! They write reviews on dsw.com, and like and comment on our Facebook, Pinterest, and Twitter pages.

THEY LOVE THEIR SHOES AND ARE NOT SHY ABOUT LETTING EVERYONE KNOW IT.

"*I am a size 10, and I have been since I was in 8th grade. Back then, everything seemed to revolve around the latest shoes—which I couldn't wear because my feet were just too big! Those cool, hip styles were never available in my size. Now I'm in my 20s, and I never have that problem—because I found DSW! My latest obsession is red ballet flats with a bow, and DSW always has my size. Thank you DSW—you are my prince charming!*"

–Patricia Kay Williams, Shoe Lover & Customer, Noblesville, IN

Even if someone wasn't always a Shoe Lover and only came to be one later in life, DSW figures prominently into an individual's conversion.

> _**I** used to be the guy who had one pair of black sneakers that I wore with EVERYTHING, until I met my girlfriend. She forced me to buy brown shoes to go with my brown belt; and that was just the start of my shoe love! Now I visit DSW weekly to buy sneakers and dress shoes in all different colors—whatever I'm in the mood for. They really set the Shoe Lover in me free!"_
>
> –Justin Hall, Shoe Lover & Customer, Hayes, VA

PART OF LOVING SHOES AND BEING FEARLESS IN YOUR CHOICES STARTS WITH HAVING A SENSE OF HUMOR AND NOT TAKING YOURSELF TOO SERIOUSLY.

In fact, DSW's SVP of Marketing Kelly Cook's sense of humor and style are essential to her shoe love and working at DSW! Her nickname, "Runway Roadkill," came from her early days as a runway model, when she wore four-inch heels the first time down the runway and totally wiped out—almost breaking her ankle. Right out of an episode of _Sex & the City_, she got right up, dusted herself off, and finished her strut down the runway. She still remembers those bright red platform shoes like it was yesterday. And they didn't stay her nemesis for long; she bought them the next day!

"*I* can remember the very first designer shoes that I ever bought, and I have DSW to thank for making it happen. I was able to combine some Rewards certificates and buy them. They were my first shoes that came with their own velvet sleeves. I still have them, and I keep them way in the back of my closet."

Monica Jean Alaniz, Shoe Lover & Customer, Penitas, TX

the TIPS

According to Bryan Dow, DSW's Creative Director & Shoe Lover, you should always ask yourself the following questions before buying a pair of shoes:

1 *Do you absolutely love them?*

2 *Are they a great value?*

3 *Do they personalize your look?*

4 *Will they last?*

5 *Do they go with your wardrobe and your style?*

It's okay to have your own personal style.

AFTER ALL, IT'S SOMETHING THAT DEFINES YOU.

1 Napoleon Dynamite's vintage Tecnica moon boots were his calling card and fans of the movie remember them fondly—they "defined" his character.

2 Diamonds are so overrated! We about died when Big proposed to Carrie with that fierce Manolo Blahnik. Who wouldn't say yes?

Speaking of defining character...

3 How about Vinny's black steel-tipped cowboy boots in *My Cousin Vinny*? Talk about iconic!

4 We still lust over the pair Rene Russo wore in the movie *The Thomas Crown Affair*; she made biker boots sexy and feminine!

5 The Dude's jelly sandals are what made him so cool in *The Big Lebowski*.

7 Who didn't love Agent 86's famous shoe phone in *Get Smart*? In fact, we want one now!

8 White platform loafers have become synonymous with Pee-wee Herman—we can almost hear Tequila playing when we see 'em!

"Keds. They bring back memories of both my childhood and my character Baby from *Dirty Dancing*. Yes, they'll always have a special place in my heart."

Jennifer Grey, Shoe Lover & Actress, Los Angeles, CA

SHOE NOTES

(LIKE CLIFF'S, BUT WAY MORE FABULOUS!)

1

Fun. Flirty. Fashionable. The three words every Shoe Lover should live by!

2

Aren't you always checking out shoes in movies? So are we! Hey—perhaps you should work here too?!

3

We agree! Rewards certificates are an outstanding way to get even better deals!

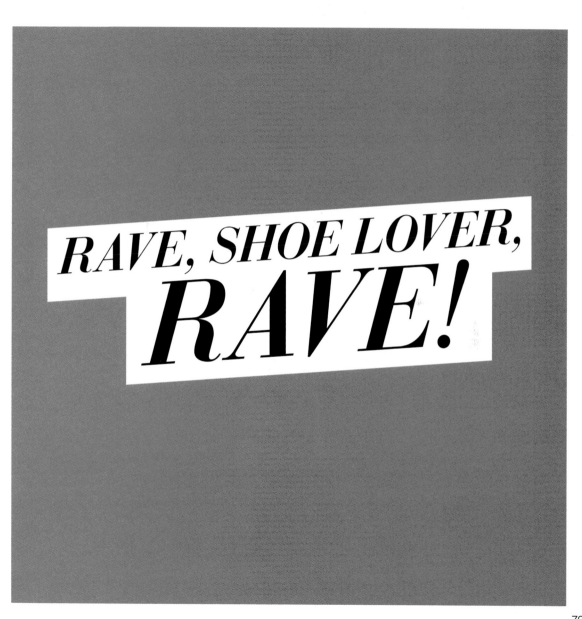

RAVE, SHOE LOVER, *RAVE!*

SHOE COUNT
40

AHMED SALAD
MANAGER OF ONLINE EXPERIENCE

NICKNAME
Barefange

WORDS THAT DESCRIBE YOUR STYLE
Smart, versatile, stylin'

CAN'T LIVE WITHOUT
A white or blue dress shirt, a tailored blazer, and
my Kenneth Cole black leather slip-ons.

FASHION FAUX PAS
I used to get all my pants tailored to look like MC Hammer back in the '90s.
Oh, and I wore turtlenecks under dress shirts. So there's *that*.

OUTRAGEOUS SHOE STORY
I grew up very poor in Balanbala, Kenya. Wanting to help my family out with finances, I began making sandals out of
old tires and sold them around town. Since I crafted them by hand, I knew they were made very well and would last a
long time. Even at the age of ten, quality was important to me. That experience shaped and grew my love of shoes!

Erin Kelly

DIRECTOR OF INTERACTIVE EXPERIENCE

NICKNAME
Marie-ski

WORDS THAT DESCRIBE YOUR STYLE
Classic, smart, chic

CAN'T LIVE WITHOUT
My Giuseppe Zanotti sandals. They're the most expensive shoes I've ever bought, but let me tell you they were SINGING to me when I saw them! (And they may or may not have their own special spot in my house, outside of my closet. Just saying.)

FASHION FAUX PAS
I'm a total T.O.F.F.I. girl (that's a tear-out-for-fashion-inspiration girl). Images of outfits, bags, tops, shoes, jeans, you name it—if I love it, I tear it out. My husband, who hates clutter, can't stand it so I hide them all around our house in shoeboxes. I can't stop—it's an obsession!

OUTRAGEOUS SHOE STORY
I am the worst packer ever. If I'm going on a seven-day trip I pack eight outfits. I know you're supposed to economize, but it's impossible for me. I once went on a two-day trip and I brought two stuffed suitcases (with five pairs of shoes). It's nuts, I know—but hey, it's all in the name of fashion!

Melissa Jenkins

STORE MANAGER, EASTON MARKET

NICKNAME
Sissy

WORDS THAT DESCRIBE YOUR STYLE
Girly, ladylike, diva-ish

CAN'T LIVE WITHOUT
A perfectly fitted black pencil skirt and a beautiful red pump.

FASHION FAUX PAS
On my wedding day, I had been going, going, going (you know how weddings are!), and I didn't really get a chance to eat. When we sat down at our reception, I took my first bite of mac and cheese and spilled it all over my beautiful, lovely, *very-white* dress. *Seriously?* It was terrible, but my Tide To-Go pen saved the day—and my dress!

OUTRAGEOUS SHOE STORY
I'm a hopeless romantic, and I'm head-over-heels in love with my husband, Matt. I have four pairs of shoes that are memories of big moments with him: in my red Nine West pumps we fell in love, in my Mojo Moxy heels he proposed, in my leopard BCBG shoes we had our engagement party, and in my something-blue Audrey Brooke sandals we got married!

NICKNAME
Vee-Gee

WORDS THAT DESCRIBE YOUR STYLE
Fun, colorful, preppy-meets-punk

CAN'T LIVE WITHOUT
A classic, clean, crisp white button-down shirt and moto boots.

FASHION FAUX PAS
I'm one of 11 children so everything I wore growing up was a hand-me-down. My older sister felt sorry for me and bought me this amazing bright yellow jumper when I was seven years old. I was so excited when she gave it to me; I threw it on faster than fast and ran out the door to school. Little did I know I had it on backwards. Everyone started calling me "Backwards Betsy." Silly me!

OUTRAGEOUS SHOE STORY
When I was in high school, all the girls (including me!) dressed the same. Same sweaters, same jeans, same shoes. I woke up one day and decided I wanted to be different. I went shopping and got this amazing pair of Keds sneakers— and that's when it all started. I paired them with dainty skirts, crazy tops, and black, cat-rimmed glasses. I ended up getting the award of Most Radical in my class, all because of those cool Keds!

WHERE'D YOU GET THOSE SHOES?

VALARA GEE
VP, STORES

SHOE COUNT
200

NATHAN UPDYKE
SENIOR MANAGER OF BUSINESS INTELLIGENCE

SHOE COUNT 12

FUNNY WHAT MEN THINK ARE A LOT OF SHOES

NICKNAME
N8

WORDS THAT DESCRIBE YOUR STYLE
Practical, consistent, classic

CAN'T LIVE WITHOUT
My three must-haves—an excellent pair of running shoes (love me some Asics), casual boots (what's up, Aston Grey?), a cool bowtie.

FASHION FAUX PAS
I used to wear brightly colored button-ups from Express—exclusively. It was excessive and it was not my proudest moment.

OUTRAGEOUS SHOE STORY
I still have the cycling shoes I was wearing when I met my wife. I got off my bike and walked toward her—problem was, the clips were still on the front of them causing me to walk unmanly, very unmanly, toward her. I guess she didn't mind, though—she said yes to a date!

SHOE COUNT **142**

Alicia Peake

MERCHANT

NICKNAME
Pooh

WORDS THAT DESCRIBE YOUR STYLE
Urban, chic, awesome

CAN'T LIVE WITHOUT
My black Matisse combat boots. Super comfy tees and a great pair of jeans, too!

FASHION FAUX PAS
I was out clubbing with some of my best friends and we were having a blast. All of a sudden, my friend realized she lost her ID. We were freaking out—we walked over five blocks to get there! After retracing our steps, we passed by a pair of heels, just lying on the sidewalk, that looked exactly like the pair my friend had on. Turns out, they were hers! We had been so consumed with finding her ID we didn't even notice she completely walked out of her shoes a few blocks back.

OUTRAGEOUS SHOE STORY
I have an obsession with a pair of shoes—only they're not my shoes, they were SUPPOSED to be for my best friend! When she was planning her wedding, I told her my gift to her would be wedding and reception shoes. Problem was, I couldn't find the ones she wanted for her reception anywhere. I looked and looked and looked, but they were nowhere to be found. I ended up getting her another pair, but I just can't let it go. I keep looking—I have hope!

JOANNA LAU
BOARD OF DIRECTORS

NICKNAME
Jo

WORDS THAT DESCRIBE YOUR STYLE
Confident, always-prepared, smart

CAN'T LIVE WITHOUT
A great pair of Ryka sneakers, black Stuart Weitzman pumps, and fun (and functional!) hiking boots.

FASHION FAUX PAS
I was working late at a computer center, crawling around on the floor and checking wires. It was a messy job so I was wearing jeans and a tee—very, very casual. My boss called to let me know some customers were on their way and they'd be there in 45 minutes. WHAT?! I ran to some nearby stores and bought a skirt, top, and killer high-heels. I got back just before they got there, changed, and it all went perfectly. *Phew!*

OUTRAGEOUS SHOE STORY
When I was first starting out in my career, my boss sent me to a How to Dress with Style class. At first, I was completely embarrassed, but I learned the value of dressing for the job you want—and, most importantly, to always have a pair of black pumps on hand!

SHOE COUNT
No one should ever count their shoes!

Jeff Bakehorn
DISTRICT MANAGER, COLUMBUS

SHOE COUNT 150

NICKNAME
Big Daddy

WORDS THAT DESCRIBE YOUR STYLE
Casual, classic, all-American

CAN'T LIVE WITHOUT
Three things: a classic, tailored, go-with-everything navy blazer (love mine from Joseph Abboud), a nice pair of flat-front gray dress pants, and a classic pair of brown Cole Haans (desk to dinner, *what?*).

FASHION FAUX PAS
I was managing a store and our CEO was due any minute. I noticed something on the ground so I bent down to pick it up and—*rip*. I tore my pants! I quickly stapled them back together, but it was still pretty noticeable. I carried papers behind my back for the walk-through (looking quite distinguished if I do say so myself) and I fooled him! It still makes me sweat when I think about it.

OUTRAGEOUS SHOE STORY
All my life I wanted to own a pair of expensive kicks. It was important to me—the quality, the craftsmanship, the leather. I FINALLY got them. A pair of insane Prada shoes that I'm so proud to own.

SHOE COUNT
110

ALLISON SUTLEY
DIRECTOR OF APPLICATIONS DEVELOPMENT

NICKNAME
Alli

WORDS THAT DESCRIBE YOUR STYLE
Classic, contemporary, cool

CAN'T LIVE WITHOUT
My Nine West oxblood snakeskin stilettos—the perfect combo of sexy and comfortable!

FASHION FAUX PAS
I'm a working mom, so there's a lot of juggling that needs to happen. One day, I had multiple meetings in the office, on top of my daughter's field trip. I was dressed for double-duty: a great blouse, wide-leg cuffed pants, and some killer stilettos. I left the office in a hurry and made it just in time for the departure of her field trip, with everyone filing into the school bus. As I was running up to the bus, my heel got caught on the cuff of my pants, and I totally face-planted in front of everyone—EVERYONE! Ouch.

OUTRAGEOUS SHOE STORY
I was all set to announce the promotion of a team member on our office staircase in front of the whole company. But five minutes before, wouldn't you know it, the heel broke off my shoe. I scrambled around the office looking for another pair (thank goodness I work for a shoe company!), but I could only find some that were a size too small. I squeezed my feet in, stood tall and proud, and wore them for the announcement AND the rest of the day.

SHOE COUNT

37½

(Lost one, but still holding out hope it turns up!)

Doug Probst

CHIEF FINANCIAL OFFICER

NICKNAME
Thunderstud (just kidding—my friends call me Probey)

WORDS THAT DESCRIBE YOUR STYLE
Clean, comfortable, classic

CAN'T LIVE WITHOUT
Every guy must own a pair of lucky white bucks—my favorites are from John Varvatos.

FASHION FAUX PAS
Early on in my career, I had to get up *really* early. To avoid waking up my wife and kids, I got dressed in the dark alternating between my cordovan wingtips and my black wingtips. One day, I got all the way to work before realizing I had two different *shoes on!* I tried hiding my feet all day to avoid the embarrassment, but people caught on *pretty* quick. I ran home at lunch to correct my error!

OUTRAGEOUS SHOE STORY
In high school, the shoe you had to have was the Nike Cortez (the red, white, and blue one from the movie *Forrest Gump*). It was cool to keep the white part pristine, but it was hard because—well, it's white. My friend introduced me to liquid shoe polish, which was the perfect, scuff-fixing solution. My dad thought I was a knucklehead for polishing my sneakers, but it had to be done—*regularly!*

89

Daniella Bonfante
MERCHANDISE SUPPORT ASSISTANT

NICKNAME
Punks (short for Punkin)

WORDS THAT DESCRIBE YOUR STYLE
Fabulous, glam, classy-meets-trendy

CAN'T LIVE WITHOUT
My statement-making Louis Vuitton tote. And my gorgeous Michael Kors black pumps—I was wearing them when I got the job at DSW!

FASHION FAUX PAS
I bought a pair of cheap platform flip-flops that were way too trendy and way too—just yuck! Too bad I wore them a couple times before realizing they were a HUGE mistake.

OUTRAGEOUS SHOE STORY
Ever since I've been working at DSW my boyfriend has become obsessed with shoes. He actually almost has more shoes than me! So basically, he's a total keeper.

Ron Allender

**SENIOR DIRECTOR,
FINANCIAL PLANNING & ANALYSIS**

SHOE COUNT

30

NICKNAME
Money

WORDS THAT DESCRIBE YOUR STYLE
Conservative, comfortable, classic

CAN'T LIVE WITHOUT
My blue-collared Banana Republic shirt. It's perfect to go from a board meeting to date night. And a great pair of brown, slip-on Cole Haan shoes and several pairs of Nike flip-flops!

FASHION FAUX PAS
When I was in seventh grade, I was in a pageant. It had all those standard competitions—suit, casual, and swimsuit—the whole nine yards. Well, the three-piece suit was three sizes too big, and I had to wear some pretty short Larry Bird shorts—it was just terrible! I've since burned all the pictures so my wife and kids don't see them. Mark my words: my sons will never go through that.

OUTRAGEOUS SHOE STORY
A few years back I was on vacation with my family. We all started talking about half marathons and my brother and wife started ribbing me that there was no way I could ever do one. I took that as a challenge. When we returned home, I bought a pair of Adidas shoes, started training my butt off, and ran the thing. My wife was amazed I went to such great lengths to prove them wrong. Frankly, I'm glad I impressed her—I need all the help I can get!

Jordan Rivchun
MANAGER OF INVESTIGATIONS

NICKNAME
Spider Monkey

WORDS THAT DESCRIBE YOUR STYLE
Comfortable, professional, current

CAN'T LIVE WITHOUT
Cole Haan shoes—yes, all Cole Haan shoes. I'm totally into that brand. Also, a great pair of jeans from Gap or Express and a striped button-down.

FASHION FAUX PAS
I was in the process of moving and no longer had a washer and dryer at my place, so I stopped over my girlfriend's (who's now my wife) house to do some laundry. I threw all my clean stuff, in addition to some shoes and other things, in a big garbage bag and set it in the hallway. I spent the rest of the night watching a big b-ball game, while my girlfriend did some errands and cleaning. The next day, I was getting ready to leave and that bag containing all my stuff? Couldn't find it. I texted my girlfriend and she wrote back that she thought it was trash and tossed it in the dumpster. So there I was, dumpster diving in my boxers. Too bad that morning was trash day. Sayonara, clothes.

OUTRAGEOUS SHOE STORY
My outfit of choice growing up? A pair of shorts and red cowboy boots. My cousins still make fun of me for it.

SHOE COUNT
100

ASHLEY SIMMONS
ASSISTANT BUYER

NICKNAME
Ash

WORDS THAT DESCRIBE YOUR STYLE
Put-together, interesting, unique

CAN'T LIVE WITHOUT
I have to have a great pair of go-to heels. Something that I can feel good in no matter what I'm wearing or where I'm going (desk-to-dinner fabulous!). And I love a cool textured jacket.

FASHION FAUX PAS
Growing up in Alabama, I dressed a little out-of-the-box and I always, always, ALWAYS stood out. Turns out it was a good thing because people started coming to me for fashion advice. I guess it pays to be unique!

OUTRAGEOUS SHOE STORY
Shoes are my vice. It doesn't matter what else is working in the fashion world, shoes are what I fixate on. Needless to say, I've definitely been known to drop some serious cash on a pair I can't live without. How much? I'll NEVER tell!

2

TAKE IT FROM
A SHOE LOVER

STYLING TIPS AND SAVVY ADVICE

FROM THE EXPERTS AT DSW

SHOE STYLING
101

From the office to date night,
ankle strap pumps have you 100%
covered. (How amazing is that
gold-studded trim?)

Levity *Kimi Pump*

7

THE JOB'S ALL YOURS

PERFECT SHOES FOR INTERVIEWS

A new job starts with your first interview, which begins with a first impression. And since you're taking those first steps with whatever you've got on your feet, what better way to make a first impression than with your shoes? Of course, there are countless elements at play when you step into an interview; the perfect shoe is just one of many that you should take into account when preparing. Whatever your chosen field may be, your shoes speak volumes about you. So take your time and scour the shopping scene to find the pair that'll make a great first impression.

> *"My friend's grandmother taught me that the three most important elements to making a good first impression are: 1) have a great haircut; 2) always smile; and 3) always wear great shoes!"*
> –Phillip Miller, Shoe Lover & Board of Directors Member, DSW

Shoes clearly make an impression. You never know what your interviewer is focusing on and what's factoring into their assessment of you during your discussion. The fact is that most people notice your shoes as one of the first elements of your persona, so be sure your shoes say precisely what you want to express about your personality. The first question you should ask yourself before picking out shoes for an interview is: "What type of company is this?" In other words, is this a conservative company or a more creative one? If it's the former, choose shoes that blend in with your outfit, that don't say too much about your personality (like, for instance, super-high glittery heels may insinuate you like to party more than work!). If you're interviewing with a company in the fashion industry, being current with your look is always important.

And if you're a creative type, interviewing for a position in a more creative field (for example, a new media position vs. a finance position), feel free to let your shoes convey your creative spirit. Just don't let what you're wearing distract your interviewer from the most important task at hand—convincing him or her to hire you!

Erin Kelly, Shoe Lover & Director of Interactive Experience at DSW, tells us that whenever you leave the house—whether it's for an important interview, another day on the job, or a big meeting—you should always pick shoes that'll make you feel confident no matter how nervous or unsure you may be feeling on the inside.

AN ESSENTIAL RULE WE MUST TELL YOU IS TO NEVER, EVER LEAVE THE HOUSE WITH THE STICKER ON THE BOTTOM OF YOUR SHOE.

We will never forget the image of the beautiful Tawny Kitean in the Whitesnake video ("Here We Go Again"), as she kicks up her gorgeous leg mid-way through the video to reveal a gorgeous pointy stiletto heel with a price tag on the bottom. Talk about a "cringe worthy" moment!

SHOES
not
TO WEAR
TO AN INTERVIEW

Crystal Kirkbride, Shoe Lover & Divisional Merchandise Manager at DSW, advises that there are certain no-nos when it comes to interview shoes:

~~athletic sneakers~~

~~evening sandals~~

~~extreme heels~~

~~glitter or metallic shoes~~

~~old or dirty shoes~~

If the company or the position you're seeking is less by-the-book and more creative, then you can be a little more inventive with your shoe choice. Your interviewer will definitely take note of your outfit, usually starting with your shoes.

> *"I have my shoes to thank for my job. I was graduating from college and attending a job fair in my college campus's quad when I realized I had run out of resumes. I told the person I was interviewing with I'd be right back and literally sprinted back to my dorm in my 2.5 inch black patent leather heels. When I got back, (in less than 5 minutes flat), my interviewer offered me the job, telling me she could tell how much I wanted the job and how I'd be a real go-getter after seeing me run in those high heels! Seven years later, I still work there!"*
>
> –Kate Humphrey, Shoe Lover & Customer, Kansas City, MO

SHOES CAN BECOME A TALKING POINT THAT BREAKS THE ICE IN AN INTERVIEW.

> *"I had a big interview in Chicago, so I went to DSW looking for the perfect shoe. I found it and wore it confidently to my interview. As I was finishing the interview, the hiring manager looked at my shoes and told me that she had the same pair. We bonded over DSW. I got the job and still work there today!"*
>
> –Della Vernsey, Shoe Lover & Customer, Aurora, IL

I have a fun interview-bonding story of my own, back when I was trying to land an in-house lawyer position at a movie studio. I was hoping to make the jump from being an associate at a big corporate law firm, to a more relaxed role. The job seemed like it would be extremely cool—especially after I met my interviewer and prospective new boss whose first words to me as I entered her office were, "love your shoes." I knew we would connect as she spoke those words, and when she got up from her desk to shake my hand, I saw she was wearing the exact same pair as me! Now that's kismet.

20-year-old Robert Clergerie wedges!

My feet are still on the ground.

I'M JUST WEARING BETTER SHOES.

Oprah Winfrey

SHOE NOTES

(LIKE CLIFF'S, BUT WAY MORE FABULOUS!)

1

Big interview? Perfectly-fitted jacket. Always smile.
Excellent pair of shoes.

2

Save the cool glitter shoes you picked up at DSW
for the dance floor. What a feeling?!

3

No matter where you're interviewing,
we've got it at DSW. One-stop shop.
It's one less thing to worry about for that big day!

SHOE STYLING
101

*A detailed gladiator takes even
your most casual shorts and
simplest skirts someplace exciting.*

Giuseppe Zanotti *Satin Flower Sandal*

8

WORK THOSE SHOES!

SENSATIONAL 9 TO 5 STYLE TIPS

The perfect shoe for an interview may not always be the perfect everyday work shoe.

The right shoe can perk up your day at work and help to change your entire outlook.

You may not realize how much your shoes say about you and your personality at work. Sometimes they might even make you the focal point of a meeting—for better or worse.

"I had an important meeting out of the office with a totally stylish executive. Because she always, always commented on my shoes, I put on my best YSL platforms and got in the taxi to go to her offices. As I got out of the taxi my heel hit the ground strangely and literally broke off. I was panicked. I looked around and as luck would have it, found myself right in front of a DSW. I went in and bought a pair of Fergie suede pumps. The first thing she said to me when I walked into her office was 'Love, love those shoes—where did you get them?' I told her and she went right out after and bought a pair. They were totally awesome and I still love them today!"

–Allison Wallach, Shoe Lover & Customer, New York, NY

BEFORE WALKING OUT THE DOOR IN THE MORNING, ASK YOURSELF IF YOUR SHOES ARE SAYING WHAT YOU WANT THEM TO SAY ABOUT YOUR PROFESSIONAL IMAGE.

"Many years ago, my colleague and I were being interviewed due to the merger of our two companies. I wore my classic wingtips, as I always do, and my colleague wore a clunkier heeled shoe. The interview was published in a magazine—and much to our surprise, the interviewer focused the entire article on the differences between our companies based on our shoe choices!"

Philip Miller, Shoe Lover & Board of Directors Member, DSW

People often associate shoe choices for work as either "fancy and uncomfortable" or "dumpy and comfortable." But there are many options that allow you to take style and comfort together to the workplace.

WEDGES

Today's wedges (like these gorgeous gems) can be way more comfortable than a pump, but just as fashionable. You still get that great heel and glamorous height, so wearing them with your tailored dresses, pencil skirts, or dress pants is completely seamless. Have a job where you're on your feet all day? Not into those blisters and bruises you get from sky-high stilettos? Just looking for a little comfort with your trends? Work the wedge, girlfriend. Work it!

BALLET FLATS

Okay, okay, we've all been there. Testing out those fabulous new heels at work and what do you know—they are just not making the cut. You're uncomfortable, you can barely walk, you feel like you might lose a toe at any minute. So, what's a girl to do? Foldable ballet flats! Genius, right? They fold up, they fit in a cute little bag, and best of all they're comfortable. Plus, they're great for errand running and commuting to and from the office.

RAIN BOOTS

Picture this: you already have your outfit planned for the workday—some great patterned skinny pants, a pretty silk top, and brand new ankle strap heels. Then, you peer outside only to find it's raining. Downpouring all over the place. You could **a)** say, who cares and wear your new shoes anyway, **b)** change your whole outfit up to match an old pair of heels you're not as worried about, or **c)** opt for rain boots. We pick **c!** And if you go the rain boots route, you can jump in some puddles—and puddle-jumping is seriously underrated.

MOCCASINS

Super comfy moccasins are your best bet if you've got a long commute. Whether you're traipsing around a big city, hopping on a bus or train, or you've just got a long drive—moccasins are absolutely the way to go. Just throw your work shoes in a fabulous tote, and get on the road in your moccasins of choice. How awesome that there are these fabulous little slipper-like shoes you can wear OUTSIDE?

WE'D BE REMISS IF WE DIDN'T TOUCH ON STYLE IN SCHOOL—AND WHAT BETTER WAY TO ILLUSTRATE THAN WITH KIDS? CHILDREN SEEM TO KNOW EXACTLY WHAT THEY LIKE AND WHAT THEY DON'T WHEN IT COMES TO SHOES (AND COUNTLESS OTHER THINGS!). AND IT'S NOT JUST COMFORT THAT THEY CARE ABOUT; STYLE IS ALSO IMPORTANT TO THEM.

"I like to wear shoes that are fun and flirty, even at work. I was starting a new teaching job a few years ago, and I wore my favorite strappy, wedge sandals for the first day. I overheard two of my new students talking after class about how they finally had a teacher with style. It made me smile and I ended up loving that job, those students and that school more than any other job I ever had before or since!"

—Terrie Lewis, Shoe Lover & Customer, Centerburg, OH

"My son, Pete, is so into shoes he almost puts me to shame! He has ten pairs and is only five years old. We were shopping for shoes recently and he saw a pair of Air Jordans. He told me, 'Those are the retired shoes, daddy. I don't want retired shoes; I want now shoes.' I was floored!"

—Tim Harpe, Shoe Lover & Director shoephoria! Center, DSW

SHOE NOTES

(LIKE CLIFF'S, BUT WAY MORE FABULOUS!)

1

9 to 5 can mean "mine to thrive" when picking up fantastic work shoes at DSW.

2

Wedges, flats, rain boots, moccasins—so many stylish work options.

3

Kids love school style, too. Our kids' shoes at dsw.com can make every kid stylish. What fun!

SHOE STYLING
101

*A shoe like this IS the outfit.
Who cares about the other
stuff—all eyes will be looking at
you strut!*

Michael Antonio *Trudi Platform Sandal*

9

SHOE LOVE AT FIRST SIGHT

WHAT TO WEAR FOR BIG NIGHTS OUT ON THE TOWN

Let's be honest—sometimes we dress more for our friends' approval than anything or anyone else. We've even heard some women admit that they care more about what other women think of their shoes than what their own boyfriends or husbands think. Who else but another Shoe Lover can appreciate the detail and thought that goes into picking just the right shoe for a night out with the girls? And we all know that sometimes a little pain is worth all those compliments.

> *"I bought the hottest shoe for a friend's wedding. I hadn't seen my girlfriends from college in a while so I was so excited to wear them. I knew they looked HOT, and even though they were a teeny-tiny bit uncomfortable (or maybe very much so!) I didn't care; I looked great. All night everyone kept complimenting me on my shoes. It was totally worth the pain!"*

Erin Kelly, Shoe Lover & Director of Interactive Experience, DSW

SPEAKING OF WEDDINGS

It makes us so proud at DSW to see so many Shoe Lovers experimenting with their shoes in a non-traditional way on their special day.

"A friend told me that I had to break in my wedding shoes, but that I should put tape on the bottoms so they didn't get scuffed up before the big day. I must have used the wrong kind of tape because a few days before the wedding when I removed the tape it left a sticky residue and everything stuck to the bottom of my shoes! Worse yet, I was getting married on an island, where there were no wedding shoes to buy! I had to order a pair online and overnight them, thank goodness DSW had my size and color!"

Elissa Phillips, Shoe Lover & Customer, Los Angeles, CA

Rain boots? *Yes!* Cowboy boots?
Of course! Converse? *Why not?!*
Your wedding is a fantastic time
to express your style through
your shoes; and it's not
just about white satin
pumps anymore.
How fun!

IT'S ALWAYS FLATTERING WHEN YOUR DATE APPRECIATES THE IMPORTANCE OF SHOES AS MUCH AS YOU DO.

Patti's come-and-get-me heels!

"*My husband knows how hard it is for me to find shoes in my size (10N), so he surprised me and bought me an amazing pair of mahogany pumps. They have little bows on the heels and are fabulous. I wear them whenever we go out on a date night.*"

Elaine Eisenman,
Shoe Lover & Board of Directors Member, DSW

"*My go-to date night shoes are the gorgeous gold, sparkly peep toe pumps I got at DSW in Easton. My husband has a special name for those shoes…but I can't tell you what it is, because it's our secret. But trust me— he likes them!*"

Patti Gilligan, Shoe Lover
& Director Learning Resource Center, DSW

PICKING THE
PERFECT DATE SHOES

1 Consider where you're going. Are you going to a hip, new steakhouse? Perhaps your first date is a church picnic or a county fair. Or a hot, new club? Or maybe watching football at a sports bar? "Where to?" is important.

2 Consider your personality. As we have said throughout, shoes are a way to express who you are. Are you classic casual? Are you super trendy? What are your favorite shoes in your closet that express your personality best? What do you have that makes you the most happy, relaxed, and comfortable?

3 Consider the whole outfit. Balance the top and the bottom with your shoes. If your outfit is somewhat tame or monochromatic in color, you can pop the shoes in a big way. If you're super dressy on the top, maybe a nude or almost invisible heel is best.

4 Put all elements together! If you are going on a date to a county fair, a long-sleeved t-shirt and boyfriend jeans paired with Converse Chuck Taylors is darling. If you are going to a hot, new club, gorgeous (yet comfortable) platforms are perfect! If you're going to a wine bar, a pair of simple black leggings and an asymmetrical black sweater paired with a pointy-toe high heel is uber glamorous.

Though they might seem worlds apart, going out on a first date is not that different from going to a job interview. You need to put your best foot forward when it comes to choosing your shoes. The extra thought that you put into what you wear—on both your body and your feet—for that special date will go a long way.

"The perfect shoes for a date with my wife are my Aston Grey lace-up boot. The special addition? A bowtie. Why, you ask? Simple. Women love bowties! Plus they are low maintenance, make you look polished, and don't fall in the sink when you are washing your hands!"

Nathan Updyke, Shoe Lover & Senior Manager of Business Intelligence, DSW

You may not realize how much attention your date will pay to your shoes, much more than your outfit. Your shoes might even be a make or break issue to your date. And because they stand out, the wrong shoe choice may very well determine whether there will be a second date. Your shoes make a personal statement about you, so you better make sure it is the right statement.

NEVER PAIR AN
EXPENSIVE
SUIT WITH A
CHEAP SHOE.

Harris Mustafa, Shoe Lover
& EVP Supply Chain Planning
& Allocation, DSW

SHOE NOTES

(LIKE CLIFF'S, BUT WAY MORE FABULOUS!)

1

Weddings. What an uber fantastic opportunity to express your own shoe style. We just love our Shoe Lovers' sense of expression on their big day!

2

The perfect venue? Sure. Great wine? OK. Hot heels? Crucial! A date's just not a date without jaw-dropping shoes.

3

Never pair an expensive suit with a cheap shoe. Quality footwear is of the utmost importance at DSW.

SHOE STYLING
101

Part saddle shoe, part modern oxford—wear it with a slim-fitting suit or colored chinos for a got-it-going-on look.

Ben Sherman *Raven Saddle Oxford*

10

A CHANGE
WILL DO
YOU GOOD

KEEPING YOUR STYLE
UP-TO-DATE

BRYAN'S TIPS FOR
KEEPING IT
"SHOE REAL"

When it comes to fashion, DSW Creative Director Bryan Dow knows his stuff. It's his job to create marketing campaigns for DSW each season (plus lead the way on all creative plans!), and he's got a fresh, fun perspective on style. Here's his advice for never falling into a shoe rut (we're sure he never has!).

"*A shoe rut? No. Such. Thing. At the end of the day, it's all about being versatile with your look—you don't always have to choose different shoes; just reinvent how you wear them! Take my absolute favorites: wingtips. I wear them with EVERYTHING—from a suit to jeans and (best of all) city shorts in the summer. The same shoes get tons of mileage, and my outfits end up being totally unique. I've always believed that shoes can define a person's personality—your spirit, your energy, and your attitude. So no matter what, don't tell the same story over and over. Be unexpected, add a pop of color to your black and brown, and try something new. A little bit goes a long way and your look will always be new and fun. And that's what I absolutely love!*"

1 **BUY WHAT YOU LOVE**
don't worry about where
you will wear them

2 **MAKE SURE
THEY FIT**

3 **BUY THEM IN MORE
THAN ONE COLOR**
wait for a sale or earn your
points to buy another pair

4 **DON'T TAKE
YOURSELF TOO
SERIOUSLY**

5 **DRESS SHOES GO
WITH EVERYTHING**
and always leave
a good impression

ABBY'S TIPS FOR

STYLE ON A BUDGET

As Producer of Fashion and Branded Content at DSW, fashion is Abby Greene's entire world. She helps execute photo shoots and commercials—plus, she's the team's designated style guru. She keeps fashion fresh here at DSW, and she does the same with her own wardrobe—especially shoes! Here's her advice for avoiding a shoe rut at all costs.

"*I* *think women are lucky; we have so many amazing styles to choose from ALL the time. My advice? Take advantage. I definitely have my favorites that I'll never retire, but I always keep my eye on new ways to do things. Here's the idea: if you love nude pumps, try one with a cap-toe or cutout. If you always wear flats, grab a pair with a pattern or print to spice things up. You don't have to change your style, just look for that added somethin-somethin. Oh, and another tip: don't let the seasons hold you back. Boots all summer? Yes. It's such a cool way to rethink your summer wardrobe. Pumps in the winter? It adds some sexiness to all those layers. Most of all, I don't think we should let predictable fashion rules define us. THERE ARE NO RULES!*"

1
START EACH SEASON WITH THE CLASSICS
boots you can wear with everything, traditional pumps, or the perfect wedge sandal

2
ADD AN UNEXPECTED SHOE TO YOUR WARDROBE
perhaps the one you thought was too trendy—go for it!

3
SIGN UP FOR REWARDS PROGRAMS
every time you shop, you get perks!

4
ADD A POP OF COLOR TO YOUR OUTFIT
with your shoes

5
DON'T BE AFRAID TO STOCK UP

But what if the only shoes you can handle on a down day are something comfortable and cozy? We all have a pair of shoes in our closet that we can't seem to throw away—even the ones that are falling apart or so out of style your friends won't be seen in public with you while you have them on your feet. Or maybe they're just your Saturday morning shoes, not really meant for public display—but yet there you are at your local Starbucks wearing them out in the open! Maybe they are your old favorite sneakers, or fuzzy boots, or even worse—flip-flops that you wear to church.

In fact, one customer told us her husband is completely guilty of this trait. For years he refused to throw away the ugliest, oldest sneakers he owned. He wore them every Saturday to work out and worse yet—he wore them without socks! Yuck! She finally decided they had to go and they mysteriously disappeared one night. He had to go out and buy a new pair. Let me tell you how happy his family is about that!

Taking the extra effort with your shoes, even when you may be feeling lazy (or forced to buy a new pair!), is the first step to getting out of that shoe rut. Great shoes make a difference and can transform the way you view yourself!

Every single shoe purchase reflects the mood you were in when you made that buy—for better or worse. One awesome style can be seen as the best purchase ever, while another pair, not so much. But for some people, no shoe—no matter how high, brightly colored, or uncomfortable it may be—is a mistake. They believe every shoe-shopping trip ends with some great pairs that were totally necessary at that particular moment in their life.

"Shoe mistake? NEVER! I don't regret a single shoe purchase. I love them all!"

—Carolee Friedlander, Shoe Lover & Board of Directors Member, DSW

SHOE NOTES

(LIKE CLIFF'S, BUT WAY MORE FABULOUS!)

1

Versatility in your look is cool. Buy shoes that can go with lots of different outfits.

2

Shoes = Pop of Color. We sell lots and lots of colors. Try them all!

3

Triple Points events are the savviest way to get more Rewards certificates. Go get 'em!

SHOE STYLING
101

Oh, the d'Orsay pump (be still our hearts)! These versatile yellow ladies pair perfectly with other brights or a crisp monochromatic look.

BCBG Paris *Jaze d'Orsay Pump*

FASHION'S MOST-WANTED

11

THE SHOES NOBODY SHOULD LIVE WITHOUT

for the
GALS

1. OH-SO-FLIRTY WEDGE SANDALS

2. I'VE-GOT-THE-POWER BLACK DRESS SHOES

3. SUPER SEXY NUDE PUMPS

4. WEAR-EVERYWHERE BALLET FLATS

5. ULTRA EDGY LEOPARD BOOTIES

6. RED-HOT PLATFORMS

7. WEEKENDS-JUST-GOT-CHIC SNEAKERS

8. STATEMENT FLAT SANDALS

9. OBSESSED-WITH BOOTIES

10. BORROWED-FROM-THE-BOYS OXFORDS

*Abby's got every single one in her closet—
are they in yours?*

2

3

5

6

8

9

10

for the GUYS

1. **WHISTLE-WORTHY WINGTIPS**

2. **ALWAYS-COOL LOAFERS**

3. **LAID-BACK SUEDE CHUKKAS**

4. **RUGGED UTILITARIAN BOOTS**

5. **STYLIN' DRIVING MOCS**

6. **TOTALLY HOT DRESS SHOES**

7. **(DARK) BLUE SUEDE SHOES**

8. **ROCKIN' BOAT SHOES**

9. **ULTIMATE ATHLETIC KICKS**

10. **ICONIC SNEAKERS**

Stock up on these and you're golden, says Bryan.

2

3

5

6

8

10

9

EQUIP YOUR KICKS.

Plain, old socks? We're over 'em. Bryan suggests looking for patterns, prints, and lots of color when it comes to wearing the right pair. Just make sure the hues complement what's going on up top (say in your shirt or tie), while still contrasting your pants and shoes. And if you break a rule, no matter—we dig that rebellious streak every now and again.

THE HANDBAG MATTERS!

Every girl needs a go-everywhere bag she loves—love, loves—says Abby. Whether you're rocking those leopard booties or sporting those sweet little oxfords, this bag should take you from a Saturday night bash to a Sunday morning brunch. Find one (or more if you're a Shoe AND Handbag Lover!) that works for your lifestyle and carry that baby with pride!

SHOE NOTES

(LIKE CLIFF'S, BUT WAY MORE FABULOUS!)

1

Oh-so-flirty wedge sandals? We've got 'em.

2

Rugged utilitarian boots? We've got 'em.

3

Perfect, fun, colorful accessories? We've got 'em.

*You want style? You want comfort?
Then you want a wedge. This one
would be insanely fun with an
equally bold outfit.*

Adrianna Papell *Boutique Lacey Wedge Sandal*

THE *RUSH* OF THE *SHOES*

12

INSPIRATION BEHIND BUILDING THE ASSORTMENT

SHOE TRENDS,

like any other fashion trends, change as fast as the wind. Building the assortment of fabulous footwear each season and highlighting these trends for all Shoe Lovers is one of the best parts of Debbie Ferrée's job. She is DSW's Vice Chairman & Chief Merchandising Officer and **this is what she does. Every day.**

"Different shoes allow us the freedom to express our personal identity, femininity, personality, and moods. From trendy to glamorous to elegant—they allow us to express a fun, flirty, fashionable attitude and make us feel like a million dollars," says Debbie. She wants DSW to have an assortment that speaks to the Shoe Lover on every level, no matter what the customer wants to express.

Debbie says in order to understand the trend, it's important to look back on the iconic shoes and shoe designers of each decade and understand the importance of their time—what stories were shoes telling in the '20s, '30s, and so on?

FASHION
OF THE DECADES.

COMPLETELY, 100%, FULLY EXPOSED.

Modernism
was the word
in the '20s.

- A new woman was born: the flapper. *Her hair was short, her make up was on, her style rocked!*

- The shoe of the decade? The Mary Jane. (Fabulous name, fabulous shoe.)

- Hollywood was obsessed with Ferragamo. He *totally* proved Italians do it better.

The '30s
and '40s?
Hollywood glam was BIG.

- Stylish, blonde, and beautiful, the bombshell that was Jean Harlow charmed *everyone*.

- Platforms. *That's all we have to say.*

- Love all things Hermès? You can thank these decades.

The *"Age of femininity"*
ruled the '50s.

- Hepburn. Monroe. Kelly. These ladies were *THE* ladies.

- Heavy, bulky shoes were out. Refined, feminine shoes (like gorgeous stilettos) were in.

- Dior's New Look spread like wildfire—and all the couture houses jumped on the bandwagon.

Power to the *youth* in the '60s.

- The shorter the skirt, the hotter the look. (Props to Twiggy on that one.)
- Closet necessities: flats, kitten heels, and cuissarde boots.
- Pucci's colorful, psychedelic prints perfectly popped.

In the '70s glam rock and *couture* stole the scene.

- Disco, baby. *Disco.*
- From wooden clogs to glitter platforms, the '70 shoe assortment was *pretty* extreme.
- Manolo. Blahnik.

Labels. Materialism. Success. Welcome to the '80s!

- Madonna said it best: We are living in a material world.
- The Gucci loafer. If you owned it, you were a big deal.
- American designers like Donna Karan, Ralph Lauren, and Calvin Klein made a name for themselves.

And from the '90s to right this very second—it's all about amazing designers like Prada, Gucci, Yves Saint Laurent, Giuseppe Zanotti, Fendi, Givenchy, and so many more.

DEBBIE SAYS:

"*Even as I review the decades now, I just love it! I love looking into the archives of all the famous, iconic designers that made shoes into art. I just get totally lost in the creative and fashionable worlds of Chanel, Valentino, Dior, Gucci, and more! With a major passion for fashion, I am influenced greatly by the 'Age of femininity,' the 1950s. The pump dominated and Dior and Hepburn were revered! We use all of our influences of creativity and fashion to build the DSW assortment of shoes season after season after season.*"

Debbie and her team have a single objective when building the assortment of shoes and trends for the season: to bring all of the beauty we see from designers into a DSW assortment so each shoe will connect emotionally with the Shoe Lover in all of us. They take inspiration from fashion to the environment— and everything in between. Debbie even has a tried-and-true model that shows all of the ways she and her team stay inspired by the world around them.

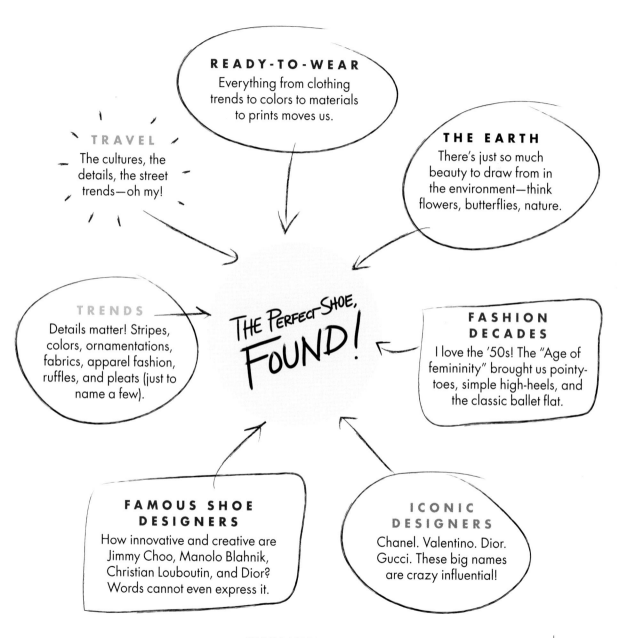

READY-TO-WEAR
Everything from clothing trends to colors to materials to prints moves us.

TRAVEL
The cultures, the details, the street trends—oh my!

THE EARTH
There's just so much beauty to draw from in the environment—think flowers, butterflies, nature.

TRENDS
Details matter! Stripes, colors, ornamentations, fabrics, apparel fashion, ruffles, and pleats (just to name a few).

THE PERFECT SHOE,
FOUND!

FASHION DECADES
I love the '50s! The "Age of femininity" brought us pointy-toes, simple high-heels, and the classic ballet flat.

FAMOUS SHOE DESIGNERS
How innovative and creative are Jimmy Choo, Manolo Blahnik, Christian Louboutin, and Dior? Words cannot even express it.

ICONIC DESIGNERS
Chanel. Valentino. Dior. Gucci. These big names are crazy influential!

ONCE THE SHOES ARE SELECTED FOR THE SEASON, QUALITY OF THE SHOES IS THE VERY NEXT FOCUS. DEBBIE TELLS A STORY OF THE INDELIBLE MARK "QUALITY" MADE ON HER IN ONE OF HER FIRST MEETINGS AS A SHOE MERCHANT.

}

"I was in a new role as a shoe merchant. I had a meeting with the CEO of a wonderful, high quality shoe company. I didn't have a lot of money to spend on shoes at the time, but wanted to make sure I was fashionable and trendy. I chose a pair of faux-snakeskin sling backs, as I knew that both snakeskin and sling backs were ultra in style at the time. Mine were cheaply made, because they were all I could afford at the time. As soon as I walked in to the meeting, he commented "Uh, nice shoes," and I instantly felt embarrassed. He worked in fashion; of course he knew quality! We have stayed friends ever since, all thanks to my very horrible shoes! It was at that time I truly understood quality and I've never forgotten it."

Debbie Ferée, Shoe Lover, Vice Chairman, & Chief Merchandising Officer, DSW

*FROM THE
POINTY-TOE PUMP
TO THE JEWELED SANDAL
TO THE ROUND-TOE FLAT—
A SHOE SAYS A LOT ABOUT YOUR
PERSONALITY AND ATTITUDE.*

What do your shoes say about you?

In picking out that perfect shoe, every Shoe Lover deserves to have a superb shopping experience—a shopping experience that makes you feel like a million bucks. Even better, a shopping experience that makes you feel like each aisle is your very own runway—aisles you can walk up and down, stopping to feel, touch, and try on all the shoes your heart desires. It helps you find the perfect trend that will show your personal style.

SHOE NOTES

(LIKE CLIFF'S, BUT WAY MORE FABULOUS!)

1

*Different shoes allow us the freedom to express our
personal identity. We couldn't agree more!*

2

*Gucci. Dior. Valentino. Ralph Lauren. Manolo Blahnik.
Prada and more. We're always inspired by you.*

3

*Getting the perfect shoe in the store—
just for you—is part art and part science.*

RAVE, SHOE LOVER, *RAVE!*

Derek Ungless
CHIEF MARKETING OFFICER

NICKNAME
Bald Babe from Britain
(courtesy of a Facebook Shoe Lover!)

WORDS THAT DESCRIBE YOUR STYLE
Sprezzatura

CAN'T LIVE WITHOUT
A gorgeous pair of O'Keeffe thick-soled shoes
I received as a gift from a friend. They are
more than shoes—they're works of art!

FASHION FAUX PAS
When I was eight, I was running late for a school
musical performance. I finally arrived, sat down in
the front row on stage, and saw that everyone had
on the polished white shoes we were supposed
to wear—except for me, of course. I forgot and
wore my dull, brown shoes. It was mortifying!

OUTRAGEOUS SHOE STORY
I grew up in the '60s in a seaside town in England.
There, you were either a *Mod* or a *Rocker*. The
Mods (which I was a part of) strictly wore bowling
shoes. Problem was, you couldn't actually buy
them—you had to "borrow" them from the bowling
alleys. Yes, I wore "borrowed" bowling shoes from
the local bowling alley. They were red and yellow
with a green cap-toe and they were awesome!

Dana Pulido

DISTRICT MANAGER, INDIANAPOLIS

NICKNAME
Day-Kay

WORDS THAT DESCRIBE YOUR STYLE
Romantic, modern, edgy

CAN'T LIVE WITHOUT
A beautifully colored tailored blazer and a killer pair of black platform pumps. Mine are Vince Camuto and I love, love, love them!

FASHION FAUX PAS
A few years back, I went on a four-day business trip that was jam-packed full of meetings. I decided to travel in my flip-flops because they're so easy in airports. Wouldn't you know it, when I started unpacking my suitcase I discovered I hadn't packed a single pair of shoes! Here I am, a massive Shoe Lover, with no shoes—just flip-flops. Luckily there was a DSW across the street (now that's fate!), so I stocked up.

OUTRAGEOUS SHOE STORY
I love vacationing in Mexico. On my last trip, I brought a pair of Michael Kors patent leather flat sandals with me for shopping. While I was wearing them, it started raining cats and dogs and my sandals were slipping on and off like crazy. I looked so goofy and insane, but I wasn't about to give up wearing my gorgeous shoes!

SHOE COUNT
200

THERESA KLADNEY
MANAGER OF PRIVATE BRANDS

NICKNAME
Tree

WORDS THAT DESCRIBE YOUR STYLE
Eclectic, risk-taker, rocker-chic

CAN'T LIVE WITHOUT
My stiletto black boots—I feel like Beyonce when I'm in them!

FASHION FAUX PAS
I buy shoes based on looks, not comfort. My leopard wedges
KILL me every time I wear them. Seriously, you'll find me in a tub of
Epsom salts afterward, but you know what? Beauty is pain!

OUTRAGEOUS SHOE STORY
Being a new mom has changed my priorities! I always loved shoes, but since I had
my daughter my favorite pair is the heels she slipped on at three and a half years
old. She looked adorable stomping around my closet—I'll never forget that image!

30

Sean Davis

ASSOCIATE CONTENT MANAGEMENT SPECIALIST

NICKNAME
Seany

WORDS THAT DESCRIBE YOUR STYLE
Crisp, clean, competent

CAN'T LIVE WITHOUT
A white collared shirt, some kind of awesome sweater (you don't have to iron your button-up if you throw a sweater on top!), and a perfect pair of skinny jeans.

FASHION FAUX PAS
When I first started wearing skinny jeans, I had a chicken-and-egg moment. I kept putting my socks on AFTER I already had my jeans on. Morning after morning, I'd slip on my skinny jeans, then I'd wobble, tilt, and fall trying to put my socks on. My dog even thought I was crazy. I finally realized the socks go on first, then the jeans—duh!

OUTRAGEOUS SHOE STORY
I was a Rewards member before I started working at DSW. One day, I got something in the mail with an image of this amazing pair of Mercanti slip-ons. I knew at that moment that I HAD to have them, and I HAD to work at DSW. So, I bought the shoes, I got an interview (wearing them, of course), and I landed the job.

Cedric Vinson

DISTRICT MANAGER, NORTH ATLANTA

SHOE COUNT 125

NICKNAME
Ced

WORDS THAT DESCRIBE YOUR STYLE
Hip-hop-influenced, trendy, edgy

CAN'T LIVE WITHOUT
A tailored suit and a nice watch.

FASHION FAUX PAS
Colored men's jeans. Trendy, right? I wore a bright orange pair to work one day (I work in retail, people!) and they looked cool. I completely forgot I was meeting some buddies at a local sports bar to watch Monday Night Football later that night. These dudes would NOT approve of my fashion decision. I almost got to the bar before I realized it, too. I ran home, changed, and went to the bar in my standard pair. *Close call.*

OUTRAGEOUS SHOE STORY
I wore my favorite Cole Haan wingtips the day I interviewed at DSW. I got the job and now those wingtips are like a trophy. I'll never, ever get rid of them!

SHOE COUNT
12

KENDRA STINEBUCK
SHOEPHORIA! CENTER ASSOCIATE

NICKNAME
Fun-sized

WORDS THAT DESCRIBE YOUR STYLE
Vintage, vibrant, slightly-boho

CAN'T LIVE WITHOUT
A great pair of dark jeans that fit perfectly and a pair of shoes that make me feel like a rockstar.

FASHION FAUX PAS
I was heading out of town on a four-day camping trip with my super trendy sisters. I was completely stressed as to what to wear. I finally went to the fabric store and bought this really beautiful material to wear tons of different ways. I thought: *this could either be a huge disaster or a really good idea*. I wore it as a sarong, top, skirt, and wrap—it actually turned out great!

OUTRAGEOUS SHOE STORY
I'm a little person, and I love it! I'm only four feet tall, and my feet are a youth size one. It's really hard for me to find adult-looking shoes in my size (like the one time I thought I was totally making out on a great pair—only to find they lit up!). Thank goodness for Nine West. My all-time favorite booties are from them, and I wear them all the time!

SHOE COUNT **40**

Roger Rawlins

SVP & GENERAL MANAGER OF DSW.COM

NICKNAME
R Squared

WORDS THAT DESCRIBE YOUR STYLE
On-trend, progressive, adventurous

CAN'T LIVE WITHOUT
My green Nike shoes. And dark wash jeans, vintage rocker shirts (love my Johnny Cash one), and a great pinstripe suit.

FASHION FAUX PAS
My first real job was at a super conservative accounting firm. I didn't have a lot of money so I went to one of those suit warehouses where you buy one suit and get like a million for free. I wore one on my first day and the entire leg seam came undone! I stapled them back together, and had to continue on with my work. I'll never forget that moment—I still have physical AND emotional scars from it!

OUTRAGEOUS SHOE STORY
I remember the first time I realized shoes were cool. I had a pair of grey lace-up dress shoes that I wore clubbing with my buddies. I danced so hard in them the soles basically turned to dust. I was gliding all over the dance floor—looking good and feeling good, too!

48

HEATHER GARREPY-SAXER
EXECUTIVE ASSISTANT

NICKNAME
Guppy

WORDS THAT DESCRIBE YOUR STYLE
Girly-tomboy, preppy, comfortable

CAN'T LIVE WITHOUT
A great-fitting pair of dark wash jeans—my absolute faves are from Levis. Everything about them is just magical. I love all my Madden Girl shoes (yeah, I've got lots of them), too! And an outfit-changing scarf is necessary.

FASHION FAUX PAS
I keep a pair of old flip-flops by the front door to take my dog out in. Because I don't put my shoes on until I'm about to leave (I was raised in a no-shoes-allowed-in-the-house kind of home), I've been known to run my dog out and then leave for work wearing the flip-flops! I've since learned, and I now keep a pair of heels at work just for those instances!

OUTRAGEOUS SHOE STORY
When I was in third grade I desperately wanted a pair of heels. My mom took me shopping and bought me this pair of white kitten-heels that I cherished—seriously, they were my prized possession! I hung onto them until I left for college and even then it was hard to let go!

SHOE ♥ LOVER

Tabatha Peterson
KIDS & ATHLETIC BUYER, AFFILIATED BUSINESS GROUP

SHOE COUNT

85

NICKNAME
Tab

WORDS THAT DESCRIBE YOUR STYLE
Sweet, sassy, confident

CAN'T LIVE WITHOUT
I loooove my Nine West platform shooties I picked up from DSW. They're perfect with dresses and skirts, and awesome with jeans. One pair of shoes that goes with every single outfit? Can't argue with that!

FASHION FAUX PAS
I was so excited for my interview with DSW that I brought my favorite blazer for the big day. As I was unpacking at the hotel that night, I noticed the hem was coming undone on my jacket—not cool. I immediately ran out, got some hem tape, and frantically ironed it back together so it would be PERFECT (I wasn't going to let a little something like an undone hem stop me!). Needless to say, I landed the job. That black blazer is now the good luck charm I'll never wear again. ('Cause, you know, I love DSW—I'm not going anywhere anytime soon!)

OUTRAGEOUS SHOE STORY
To celebrate a promotion, I bought myself a fancy pair of Cydwoq shoes. They were so awesome, I wore them every chance I could. I had them on at a shoe show in Chicago and made a stop at Steve Madden's booth—and do you know who was there? Steve Madden himself! And guess what? He smiled at me, looked down, and said, "Nice shoes." Let me repeat that: THE Steve Madden complimented MY shoes. Now that's when you know you've made it!

MIKALAH MILTON
DISTRIBUTION CENTER

NICKNAME
Kala

WORDS THAT DESCRIBE YOUR STYLE
Bright, different, fantastic-and-loud

CAN'T LIVE WITHOUT
My leather moto boots from Bandolino—I can wear them with anything!

FASHION FAUX PAS
I was waitressing at a bar and the place was packed. The music was up and everyone (including me!) was dancing and having an awesome time. I was really getting into it when I heard a huge rip and felt a gust of wind—I was in trouble! I ran into the kitchen, threw on a red apron to cover things up, and went back out to get my groove on.

OUTRAGEOUS SHOE STORY
Before going out, my girlfriends and I stopped at the supermarket. I was wearing these gorgeous stilettos and this guy was totally whistling at me and checking me out as I walked in the store. I tried to ignore him and play it cool—but I was also kind of strutting my stuff in my hot heels thinking, "Yeah, he's into me. I look good." Just when I thought I was working everything perfectly, I bit it—like, completely wiped out! I got up acting like I MEANT for that to happen (which, of course, I didn't). So, so embarrassing. That'll teach me to show off!

COURTNEY MCARTOR
SENIOR GRAPHIC DESIGNER

NICKNAME
Court

WORDS THAT DESCRIBE YOUR STYLE
Cute, comfy, sassy

CAN'T LIVE WITHOUT
LBP (Little Black Pump)—it's a must-have closet staple—my go-to shoe that makes me feel great! My favorite pair are from Kelly & Katie. Also, an LBD (Little Black Dress). The one I always reach for has a ruffle down the front and an empire waist—clean and classy.

FASHION FAUX PAS
My first job out of college? DSW! When I started, my style was pretty limited (limited in that I wore Doc Martens EVERY SINGLE DAY). My boss took me to lunch one day, but first made a detour at our local DSW store to surprise me with a new pair of shoes! He said if I was going to be a DSW Shoe Lover, I had to look the part.

OUTRAGEOUS SHOE STORY
Right after my now-husband proposed to me, I went shopping for my wedding shoes. My heart was set on a pair of green suede flats, but my size was nowhere to be found. I ended up settling for some white peep-toes with some adorable shoe clips that totally jazzed them up. And then one day, out of nowhere, I stumbled across THE green suede flats in my size. I did what any girl would do and bought them too! I wore both pairs on my wedding day, taking double the pictures. My husband said he was good with it—as long as I didn't take the second set of pics with a second husband. Yep, I chose the husband, *and the shoes*, wisely!

Dave Crawford

VP OF STORE PLANNING & CONSTRUCTION

NICKNAME
Davey

WORDS THAT DESCRIBE YOUR STYLE
Upbeat, classic, current

CAN'T LIVE WITHOUT
My classic lace-ups in black and brown from Allen Edmonds—they go with EVERYTHING. I like a good and crisp long-sleeve button-up, too.

FASHION FAUX PAS
I was in a meeting at my old job and for some reason there was a lot of nervous energy going on. I started madly tapping my pen on the table. The guy across from me ended up commenting on how much I liked my pen and that I should probably take a look at my shirt. I then realized I splattered blue ink all over my face, glasses, AND shirt. Not my finest moment!

OUTRAGEOUS SHOE STORY
My wife and I were tailgating at an OSU game when a friend of hers asked where I worked. When I told her DSW she said I should have married her instead—I almost spit out my drink!

Bill Jordan
CHIEF LEGAL COUNSEL

NICKNAME
The General

WORDS THAT DESCRIBE YOUR STYLE
Conservative, professional, traditional

CAN'T LIVE WITHOUT
My wingtips are my favorite shoes. A great pair of jeans and a killer tie are necessary, too.

FASHION FAUX PAS
I flew into Delaware late one night for a big court case next morning. I was tired, exhausted, and ready to crash when I found out the airline lost my luggage. *Great.* I had no suit, no shoes, no nothing. The hotel brought me a waiter's uniform, butler's tie, shirt, and shoes. NOTHING fit, but I had to wear it all to court the next morning, looking like a fool. The opposing party was someone who was also in the retail business, so I was completely mortified. I looked like Bozo the Clown!

OUTRAGEOUS SHOE STORY
My father was employed at a shoe company when I was growing up, and worked hard to provide for us. One day he came home with a surprise for my brother and me—Air Jordans for both of us! I'll never forget it. It was like Christmas and our birthdays rolled into one—times a thousand!

Lina Lopez-Varona

AREA MANAGER, SOUTH FLORIDA & PUERTO RICO

NICKNAME
Ninita (Little Girl)

WORDS THAT DESCRIBE YOUR STYLE
Sophisticated, fashionable, on-trend

CAN'T LIVE WITHOUT
Every woman needs a killer LBD—one that works day to night and makes you feel slim and confident. Also, a pair of basic black pumps—my faves are from Marc by Marc Jacobs.

FASHION FAUX PAS
One day at our store, I walked past something that completely snagged my pants. I couldn't leave so I had to safety pin them and wrap my scarf, *cleverly,* around the tear. At the time I thought it looked crazy, but customers kept complimenting me on the originality—hey, innovation is part of fab fashion!

OUTRAGEOUS SHOE STORY
I'm a total shopaholic. Shopping's my therapy! I always wanted a pair of designer shoes, and then I found THE ones. They were a stunning pair of Gucci pumps and I was in love! They were way more than my budget could handle, so I had to leave them at the store. *Sigh.* But, I kept thinking about them, and thinking about them, and thinking about them until I finally snapped and bought them. In order to justify it, I wouldn't let myself shop for 30 long, *boring* days—worth it!

SHOE COUNT

300

Jeanie Schottenstein

WORDS THAT DESCRIBE YOUR STYLE
Classic and casual

CAN'T LIVE WITHOUT
A comfortable pair of black flats.

FASHION FAUX PAS
I have no regrets! Fashion's always changing, so every season is a chance to reinvent yourself and change things up.

OUTRAGEOUS SHOE STORY
Jay can't walk by a shoe store without going in. He LOVES to shop. I've just learned to live with it—you can't get between a man and his shoes!

Jay Schottenstein

CHAIRMAN, DSW

WORDS THAT DESCRIBE YOUR STYLE
Casual and relaxed

CAN'T LIVE WITHOUT
A great pair of walking shoes with rubber bottoms and some cool socks.

FASHION FAUX PAS
Walking out of a shoe store without shoes—that's the ultimate faux pas!

OUTRAGEOUS SHOE STORY
The first time I went to Paris I spent over three hours in a shoe store, trying on every single pair. Jeanie wanted to kill me!

3

THE MAGIC BEHIND THE CURTAIN

WHY THERE'S NO PLACE LIKE DSW

13

THE SECRET BEHIND SHOE LOVE

CREATING A FORMULA FOR SUCCESS

> *"From the first day I started at DSW, I knew I had found my home. And because I was so certain that I had made it, I made a pledge to never again wear anything but DSW shoes (...of course, I'll wear clothes, too!)."*

Mike MacDonald, Shoe Lover & President & CEO, DSW

What is the 'secret sauce' that makes both employees and customers embrace shoe love and keep coming back for more?

Kendra Stinebuck, shoephoria! Center Associate & Shoe Lover from Columbus says it best: "Do what you love and you will never have to work again."

EVERYONE WHO WORKS AT DSW IS OBSESSED WITH SHOES. WHEN YOU WALK IN THE DOORS OF OUR HEADQUARTERS IN COLUMBUS, OHIO, YOU'RE IMMEDIATELY STRUCK BY THE FACT THAT SOMETHING SPECIAL IS INDEED GOING ON HERE. IT'S OBVIOUS THAT THIS IS AN EXCEPTIONALLY FUN PLACE TO WORK—AND SHOE LOVE PERMEATES EVERYWHERE.

"What makes DSW different is the people who work there live the brand's lifestyle. They just all love shoes!"

–Jay Schottenstein, Shoe Lover & Chairman, DSW

DSW STRIVES EVERYDAY TO BE AMERICA'S FAVORITE PLACE FOR SHOES—AS WELL AS AMERICA'S FAVORITE PLACE TO WORK. THEY DO THIS BY LIVING THEIR VALUES EACH AND EVERY DAY, FOR THE BENEFIT OF THEIR CUSTOMERS AS WELL AS FOR EACH OTHER.

PASSION

BRING POSITIVITY, HAPPINESS, AND LOVE TO
ABSOLUTELY EVERYTHING YOU DO! GRAB THE UNEXPECTED
BY THE HORNS AND EMBRACE IT LIKE CRAZY.

66

One customer called the Saturday before Christmas Eve. He asked if we would open the store 30 minutes early so his wife could be the only person in the store—so she could feel like Julia Roberts in Pretty Woman. Of course, we agreed. The two of them arrived, shopped the store alone, and she walked away with not just the right new pair of shoes—but also the memory of a lifetime.

Laura Bair, Shoe Lover & Store Manager, DSW

99

> 66

I had a customer who found a great deal on a pair of UGG boots in our Polaris store and bought them to wear to her birthday party. Well, somehow the security tag went home on the boot and when she realized it she was already home and her party was the next day. She panicked and called me at the store. I told her not to worry, I would take care of the security tag before her party. I felt so badly, I told her to leave the boots in the box at her front door and I drove out to her house early the next morning (80 miles away!) and removed the tag before she woke up. I also left her a birthday note with a DSW Gift Card inside. She called me the next day to say thank you and said I saved her special day!

Jason Kondziela, Shoe Lover & Purchase Order Specialist, DSW

99

COLLABORATION

AN OPEN ENVIRONMENT MAKES ALL THE DIFFERENCE.
WHEN SHOE LOVERS WORK TOGETHER SOME PRETTY GREAT
DECISIONS AND EXCITING IDEAS ARE SURE TO HAPPEN!

66

Recently, I encountered a customer who had fallen on hard times. She was living in a shelter close to our store and was going on interviews to try to get a job. She found a perfect pair of shoes for her interviews, but didn't have enough money to buy them yet; so she asked us to put them on hold. She would save a little each week; however, the time came when we could not put them on hold anymore, and she still didn't have enough money. When I heard her story, I just bought her the shoes. She was so touched. She said my gesture made her feel human again, that someone took the extra effort and helped her out when she needed it most.

Sam Spencer, Shoe Lover & Store Manager, DSW

99

> *We have a tradition when one of our colleagues is promoted. To celebrate them, EVERYONE in the entire home office gathers around our central staircase. When the newly promoted associate is walking up the stairs, everyone claps and cheers for them. It's special. It's fun. It's moving. It makes a big company feel small and intimate.*

Derek Ungless, Shoe Lover & EVP & Chief Marketing Officer, DSW

WAY TO GO, SHOE LOVERS!

HERE'S JUST A SNIPPET OF DESERVING ASSOCIATES GETTING THEIR PROMOTION ON. *THOSE SMILES? THOSE HUGS? THOSE GORGEOUS FLOWERS?* POSITIVELY PRICELESS.

In 2009, the word "Passion" was added to DSW's core values of "Accountability, Collaboration, and Humility."

This may not be immediately clear when a customer initially walks into a DSW store, since it is an assisted, self-select model of shopping (but the values are the magic of DSW). Your inner Shoe Lover is free to touch and feel, try on, and walk in as many pairs of shoes as your heart desires. And if you need anything at all, the Shoe Lovers who work at DSW are available.

"*I rushed into the 34th Street store in NYC to find a very specific pair of shoes I saw on dsw.com. I needed them for an awards gala I had to attend in a few days. I wasn't in the store more than five minutes before Tosin (sales associate) approached and asked if she could help. She grabbed an iPad, searched for the shoe, found it in New Jersey! At first I was totally disappointed to walk out of the store without the shoe in-hand. But Tosin got on the phone, placed the order, AND found I had an unused $10 Rewards certificate! The shoes arrived in time for the gala. Bless her, she not only saved me money but it really touched my heart that she did it all so effortlessly and with a smile!*"

–Kelly Ann Turner, Shoe Lover & Customer, Brooklyn, NY

The shoes are out on display, with available sizes all stacked clearly underneath. Customers are free to try on as many pairs as they want, without having to ask anyone for help. Plus, each store has an extensive clearance section—which always serves up the opportunity to find some unbelievably great deals.

The stores are filled with Shoe Lovers and shoes—it doesn't get better than that.

"*I may have a slight obsession with clearance shoes. When I enter a DSW, I walk straight to the clearance racks where I check for my size. Because I am a Marine wife, I'm always on the lookout for shoes in the colors red, white, and blue. I recently found the most adorable pair of red, white, and blue wedges that were marked down too; plus I had a Rewards certificate. So I walked out of the store with them practically free. Nothing makes me happier!*"

–Kara Willemsen, Shoe Lover & Customer, Beavercreek, OH

There's no pressure at our stores—no hard selling sales staff, you can feel free to find-it-yourself, try it on, and fall in love with SHOES, SHOES, SHOES! All DSW stores have a breathtaking assortment of designer brands on display that are organized by type of shoe to allow shoppers to compare easily. Want a biker boot? Great! They are all displayed together. You can try on a few, compare fit, style, and price without running all over the store looking for different brands and styles.

Each and every day, a sale is made that elicits a great story about shoe love. They all have common plots: a customer makes a request to a manager or to associates, and those DSW employees take it upon themselves to accommodate that request. There's no running it up the chain of command, no store policy for these types of requests. It's the store managers who go out of their way to make a special shoe experience for their customer (as we mentioned before, these four values are the ingredients in the "secret sauce" that makes DSW a special place to both work and shop).

> *"I read every single customer compliment and complaint our stores receive. The stories are filled with passion and true shoe love. For the customer that has to have THAT shoe, we do whatever we can to find it. And when we receive a complaint, we recover immediately. How we respond tells the customer everything. Our stores and our associates make me proud to come to work every day!"*

Carrie McDermott, Shoe Lover & EVP Stores & Operations, DSW

Though some of the 'nut and bolts' of the business have changed, these four values remain constant. And this intense focus on customer experience improves the actual shopping experience and store design.

> ❝*Very early on, when we opened a store in a new city, we had people coming in and buying multiple pairs of the same shoes, like kids in a candy store. Our grand openings were crazy! People couldn't believe how many shoes we had at such great prices.*❞

Rick Smith, Shoe Lover & Former Merchant, DSW

DSW has always been known for low prices on designer shoes. A new store design was tested a few years ago based on customer needs. The customers loved the new "warehouse cool" design. The store aisles were widened and rearranged so that the customer's view of all the merchandise was unobstructed from the entrance. Customers asked for more seating and mirrors; they were both added. In fact, more mirrors were placed everywhere, so that customers who wanted to admire their shoes didn't have to wander around the store looking for a place to check themselves out!

> *"We wanted aisles big enough so customers could select shoes without bumping into the person behind them,"*
>
> —Dave Crawford, Shoe Lover & VP of Store Planning & Construction, DSW

In addition to improving store layout and design, DSW has also found a way to ignite the passion of the modern Shoe Lover through a variety of marketing programs, social networking, and numerous ways to shop (in store, online, and mobile). At the end of the day, it's all about getting the Shoe Lovers their shoes. That's where the magic happens.

DSW HAS ALSO
TO IGNITE THE
THE MODERN

"*Recently, I visited DSW in Miami with my 92-year-old mother, who had recently had surgery on her leg and mobility was a problem. She insisted on no wheelchair, so I ran into the store to browse alone while she waited in the car. To my delight, I found seven pairs of shoes she might like—what to do? Glenn (sales associate) asked if he could help and I told him my situation and offered to buy them all, and return or leave a credit card with him while I had her try on all seven pairs. Without hesitation, he offered to accompany me to the car and conduct a fitting in the parking lot; it made my mother's day! The very next day my mother asked if we could go back and buy another pair; she said she had never before had such amazing customer service in her 92 years! …I asked if she even needed more shoes. She said she didn't, but she just HAD to see Glenn again. And guess what? She bought another pair!*"

—Magda Sossa, Shoe Lover & Customer, Fernandina Beach, FL

FOUND A WAY
PASSION OF
SHOE LOVER

When building a new home office a few years ago, it was in keeping with the same warehouse cool approach as the stores. Most importantly, the home office would reflect DSW's core values.

> "*Everyone's office is the same size—10x11—which we feel emphasizes the core value of Humility. All of the offices have a glass wall (i.e., there are no secrets about who's meeting with whom), which highlights the sense of Collaboration. The home office is cool but isn't extravagant. If we built a palace, then we couldn't pass value on to our customers: and therein lies our Accountability. And finally, the building is filled with shoes and Shoe Lovers everywhere! There's a lot of passion for our business. Everyone who enters even gets a tote bag emblazoned with the words, 'I am a Shoe Lover'—thereby showing our Passion.*"
>
> – Doug Probst, Shoe Lover & EVP & Chief Financial Officer, DSW

> "*When I joined DSW, I was 57 years old. Since I've been here, I've celebrated four birthdays. Now I'm 53! Wow, how the time has flown. That's what happens when you love your job!*"
>
> –Mike MacDonald, Shoe Lover & President & CEO, DSW

SHOE NOTES

(LIKE CLIFF'S, BUT WAY MORE FABULOUS!)

1

Do what you love and you'll never have to work again. I guess that means we're not working at all!

2

Our stores are filled with shoes and Shoe Lovers. Doesn't get much better than that.

3

Passion. Accountability. Collaboration. Humility. It's the way we do what we do.

SHOE STYLING
101

When it comes to Converse, there are no rules. Chuck Taylors seven days a week? Yes. Chuck Taylors for weddings? Double yes.

Converse *Chuck Taylor All Star Sneaker*

14

STORIES FROM THE FASHION FRONT

HELPING SHOE LOVERS FIND THEIR BLISS

The Shoe Lover's shopping experience at DSW resonates from the service philosophy centered on serving fellow Shoe Lovers. Simply put: the people that work at DSW love shoes. They are what they seem, Shoe Lovers instilling their love of shoes to the customers they serve.

"From day one, DSW has always believed in delivering great brands at great prices at a great value to our customers."

– Jay Schottenstein, Shoe Lover & Chairman, DSW

The combination of the self-service store layout and the knowledgeable and friendly sales staff creates a laid-back and relaxed environment. It's one that allows customers to feel free to wander, try on, and ultimately buy fabulous shoes at an awesome value—on top of using an exclusive offer or Rewards certificate. Plus, there's no pressure and no stress at checkout.

Of course, the most important part of shoe love at DSW is the experience inside the stores. While the vast amount of shoe brands (over 400) and sizes doesn't hurt, it truly is the personal engagement that makes customers come back for more. And when they do, they often share their special shoe moments with the associates at DSW—especially those lucky enough to be in on Shoe Struck (shhh—it's a surprise; but you'll know when it happens), who participate in a Frenzy Alert, or who receive their first DSW Rewards certificate in the mail. All of this combined is what transforms a shoe shopper into a Shoe Lover at DSW.

Now, each and every associate at DSW, from the employees in the shoephoria! Center (DSW customer service call center) to the associates in the stores, is hired because:

THEY LOVE SHOES
THEY LIVE BY DSW VALUES
THEY LOVE TO SERVE ALL SHOE LOVERS

"We know that 'one size does not fit all' when it comes to service. A busy mom on her cell phone who knows exactly what she wants to buy and has only ten minutes to do it needs a different level of service than a bride-to-be who is desperately trying to pick out the perfect shoe for herself and matching bridesmaid shoes for her bridal party."

Carrie McDermott, Shoe Lover &
EVP Stores & Operations, DSW

MADDEN GIRL
$29.95
COMPARE AT $40.00

MORE
COLORS
available

SAM EDELMAN SE BOUTIQUE
$69.95
COMPARE AT $??.00

MORE
COLORS
available

Every customer enters DSW with different needs. It is the associate's job to determine that need and respond to each customer accordingly.

Serving customers like this every day generates story after story of shoe love. Some customers may come in thinking they want one thing and completely change their minds while shopping. This is when the associates are always watching and listening in case a customer needs something or has questions.

All of these stories have one thing in common; they are being told by a Shoe Lover about helping a fellow Shoe Lover. Some of these stories make us laugh, others make us cry, but all of them come from the same place: shoe love!

"I *was walking up and down the aisles at DSW, trying on a couple different shoes. When I came back to where I had been sitting, I couldn't find the shoes I wore in. I glanced down the aisle and I saw a woman who had tried on my shoes and was wearing the ones I had worn into the store. Not only that, she was admiring herself in the mirror! We both started laughing when we realized she was going to try to buy my shoes!"* —Wendy Vanover, Shoe Lover & Customer, Toms River, NJ

"I *was putting a shoe away when someone tapped me on my shoulder. She asked if I remembered her, and I did, of course; she had been in the prior month to find a shoe for her prom. She had a unique size foot to fit so it took a while. She had come back to see me to say thank you for taking the extra time, and let me know that she had won 'best dressed' at her prom. She hugged me and thanked me again. It made my day!"* —Kris Vanden Top, Shoe Lover & Assistant Operations Manager, DSW

"*We* recently had a customer come into the store with a prosthetic leg. He was a war veteran and told us his story about coming home after he was injured, and now needed shoes. Another customer overheard his story and asked if he could pay for his shoes, anonymously. He gave me his credit card and I ran it through. I then told him that a customer was so touched by his story he wanted to pay for his shoes. The war veteran began to cry, which then made me—and everyone else at the register cry as well." —Stephanie More, Shoe Lover & Assistant Store Manager, DSW

"*We* have a customer and her daughter who would visit our store every Saturday for their mother-daughter bonding experience. Well, the mother became ill and had to have treatments that kept her at home. So her daughter would bring her iPad to her house and they would visit dsw.com every Saturday until she was well enough to leave the house. There they both indulged their love for shoes in the virtual world!" —Mary Kim, Shoe Lover & District Manager, DSW

"**When I first started at DSW, I quickly observed that if we did a better job of serving our customers in stores, spending the time to listen and find what they needed, we could create more loyal customers who want to come back for more.**"

—Carrie McDermott, Shoe Lover & EVP Stores & Operations, DSW

SHOE NOTES

(LIKE CLIFF'S, BUT WAY MORE FABULOUS!)

1

We know that "one size doesn't fit all" when it comes to service. All types of Shoe Lovers need all types of service. And we're totally okay with that!

2

One of the best parts of working in a DSW store is hearing tons of shoe stories from our customers.

3

Shoe Struck? Sounds fun.

SHOE STYLING
101

*Rolled denim? Check.
Button-up and tie? Check.
Ruggedly awesome lace-up
boots? Check, check, check.*

Aston Grey *Rockcastle Boot*

15

YOU WORK FOR DSW?

ASSOCIATES' ACCOUNTS OF WORKPLACE ENVY

"*From the day I accepted my current job as CEO of DSW, my wife and I literally felt like rock stars whenever we mentioned that I worked at DSW. From the Shoe Lover at the local market to the cashier at the carwash, to the woman at the Department of Power who hooked up our lights for the new house, even our new neighbors—everyone understands the magic of shoe love.*"

Mike MacDonald, Shoe Lover & CEO, DSW

EVERYONE WHO WORKS AT DSW TELLS STORIES ABOUT THE REACTIONS THEY GET FROM PEOPLE WHEN THEY TELL THEM WHERE THEY WORK. THEY FEEL A LITTLE LIKE CELEBRITIES. EVERYWHERE THEY GO, PEOPLE WANT TO TELL A STORY ABOUT THEIR OWN, OR A FRIEND'S, OR A FAMILY MEMBER'S FAVORITE SHOES. THEY SHARE TALES OF SHOE OBSESSIONS, THEIR SHOES-GONE-BAD, AND THE PAIR THAT THEY CAN'T THROW AWAY.

"I was stuck in an airport on a delay to go home, and everyone else at the gate was incredibly grumpy. I started chatting with a man waiting for our flight; he got so excited when I told him where I worked. He unzipped his carry-on suitcase right there in the middle of the floor and started pulling stuff out of it! He grabbed his favorite shoes from DSW. It was so funny to see this grown man unpacking his suitcase to show me his shoes amidst all the cranky passengers delayed at the airport!"

Linda Canada, Shoe Lover & SVP Merchandise Planning & Allocation, DSW

*"**I** was pumping gas at a nearby station once when a woman spotted me from her car. She asked me where I got my boots, and I told her DSW. She was so excited when I told her I worked there that she came to my store the very next day and bought the same pair!"*

Tammy Culpepper, Shoe Lover & Sales Associate, DSW

*"**A** friend of mine uses me as his DSW wingman. He's always bragging to girls that his best friend works at DSW. He even calls me from bars with dates and puts me on the phone with a girl he likes to tell her I work there. I can't tell you how many girls I've gotten him second dates with because of my job!"*

Cedric Vinson, Shoe Lover & District Manager North Atlanta, DSW

"*Walking into DSW on Cinco de Mayo, it was just another freelance day. I knew there was a little celebration happening in the afternoon, but that was about it. Later at the party, I looked around and everyone was having so much fun—snapping pictures, snacking on tasty churros, beating that giant shoe piñata to a pulp. Then it hit me—I HAD to work here. At first it was all about the shoes (my god, the shoes!), but there was so much more to DSW than that. A few months later I was hired on full time, and I've never looked back.*"

– Rachel Dillon, Shoe Lover & Senior
Copywriter, DSW

take a
SWING

"Of course I get a little teary-eyed when I look at its shattered remains— that shoe piñata was my baby!"

– Heather Marr, Shoe Lover &
Art Director, DSW

"*A colleague and I were on a plane on our way to the big DSW Store Manager Conference. We talked the entire flight about how excited we were to see all the other store managers and what shoes we were going to*

Pat O'Connor, Shoe Lover & Store Manager, DSW

---

wear to every event all week. The man seated next to us finally asked what we were talking about. When we told him we work at DSW he got so excited, pulled up his suit pant leg to show us his socks he bought at DSW!"

SHOE NOTES

(LIKE CLIFF'S, BUT WAY MORE FABULOUS!)

1

You work where? We just love telling people where we work.

2

"I would not have a paycheck left if I worked there."
One of the more common responses.

3

You know how when you meet a comedian you want them
to tell you a joke? We get it! We love hearing people's fun
shoe stories when we tell them where we work.

CONCLUSION

As I read the pages of *Do You Speak Shoe Lover?* I can't express enough how much pride I feel. I have had the pleasure of meeting lots and lots of Shoe Lovers who work at DSW since I've been CEO. I'm always impressed by the amount of passion they have for our business—the business of serving other Shoe Lovers.

I remember my initial discussions about potentially leading DSW as its CEO. This was in 2008. I was already a CEO at another retailer—it was a great position at a good company. However, I must admit—even though I had that great position, I became excited as I learned more about the things that made DSW a special retailer:

> *Their stores had an impressive selection of shoes.*

> *They had fantastic everyday discount pricing.*

> *They had shoes for just about anyone's budget and desire.*

> *Customers didn't have to wait on someone to bring them their selection.*

> *Men and women could also pick up bags, belts, socks, and other great accessories at the same time.*

> *DSW had an awesome loyalty program, DSW Rewards, so customers could earn perks!*

> *The employees seemed to enjoy what they do.*

But what impressed me the most? The fact that DSW customers actually enjoyed the shopping experience and talked with one another while they were shopping. So, it's easy to understand when I say what began as a mere curiosity, as I learned more and more about DSW, quickly became an obsession. I wanted the job as CEO of DSW and I didn't want anyone else to get *my job!*

Guess what? Six very long months later, I believe I self-actualized! It was on this day that I received the call from Jay Schottenstein, offering me the position of CEO at DSW Designer Shoe Warehouse.

Since that day, I've been in our stores or our home office every week. I think the coolest part of working at DSW is that no matter whether you are standing in one of our stores or in our home office, you need only wait a few seconds and you'll hear someone, somewhere, laughing. It's a great thing. It's just a little sign that people enjoy working here. And I just love being a part of it.

It's been over four years—over one thousand, four hundred and sixty *best days of my life*—and I still love being the CEO of DSW.

I guess you could say…I *definitely* speak Shoe Lover.

Mike MacDonald,
Shoe Lover & President & CEO, DSW

the LANGUAGE OF SHOE LOVE

Shoe Love noun [shoo luhv]

An emotional, uncontrollable feeling that shakes you to the core when encountering heels, boots, wedges, wingtips, and the like.

"Sure, love's good. But, shoe love? That's epic."

Shoe Lover noun [shoo luhvr]

One who has an over-the-top obsession for footwear. He or she has been known to dip into savings to satisfy shoe needs.

"Mortgage, schmortgage. I need new stilettos— I'm a Shoe Lover, after all."

DSW Rewards noun [dee/es/duhb-uhl-yoo ri-wawrds]

The program of all programs—Shoe Lovers get exclusive perks like points, promos, style tips, free shipping, and so much more.

"DSW Rewards is the hottest thing since sliced bread."

Premier Member noun [pree-meer mem-ber]

A Shoe Lover who's earned their keep and has earned 6,000 points in a year. Shoe shopping's totally their side job.

"Dude, you're a Premier member? You're like, a celebrity or something."

shoephoria! Center noun [shoo-fawr-ee-uh-! sen-ter]
You know that O-M-G-I-got-exactly-what-I-was-looking-for
feeling when you find the shoe of your dreams?
This is the team that makes that happen.
**"I called shoephoria! Center; they found
my boots. I asked them to marry me."**

Shoe Struck verb [shoo struhk]
Shhhhh—this is a big, huge, monstrous thing that's a big, huge,
monstrous secret. Want in on it? Ask one of our Facebook Fans.
**"Shoe Struck is the secret; DSW's
Facebook page is the answer."**

National Shoe Lover Day
noun [nash-uh-nl shoo luhvr dey]
The day the earth stands still and all the Shoe Lovers
of the world come together, hold hands, sing songs, and buy shoes.
**"National Shoe Lover Day's coming up!
I'm going to take off the whole week
and celebrate the heck out of it."**

Free Shoes Friday noun [free shooz fr-eye-day]
The very best kind of Friday; a weekday where Shoe Lovers stalk @DSWShoeLovers on Twitter, answer trivia, and win free shoes.
"It's just not the weekend unless it starts with Free Shoes Friday."

Free Shoesday noun [free shooz-day]
The best way to spend a Tuesday; a weekday where Shoe Lovers hang around the DSW Designer Shoe Warehouse Facebook page, answer trivia, and win free shoes.
"This week was all Mondays 'til Free Shoesday came around."

Wedge noun [wej]
Solid-heeled silhouette with a cult following and major glam factor, most commonly spotted on spring sandals.
"Your sundresses want to know: where have these wedges been all your life?"

Stiletto noun [still-eh-toh]
The queen of all women's shoes; a high, slender heel that makes any woman feel like a knockout.
"When things get tough, the tough put on stilettos."

Bootie noun [boo-dee]

A sassy women's shoe; heeled or flat, rugged or dressy, and hitting right around or a bit above the ankle.

"It's time someone showed some leg around here. Hand me those booties!"

Riding Boot noun [rahyd-ing boot]

Classy meets comfortable; a cure-all for the everyday fall, winter, or spring outfit; a low-heeled, knee-high boot that's ridiculously flattering with skirts, skinnies, and pretty much anything else.

"You can take my land, but you can never take my riding boots."

Frenzy Alert noun [fren-zee uh-lert]

A DSW post that means it's time to chime in on Facebook to score a surprise like free Shoe Lover swag; or, when the DSW news feed starts going crazy following such an announcement.

"Whoa—my post from 10 seconds ago is already buried under this Frenzy Alert!"

PHOTO CREDITS

ABOUT THE AUTHOR

Linda Meadow is the author of the popular *City Baby LA* series, founder of gurumommy.com, and a self-proclaimed Shoe Queen. She resides in Los Angeles with her husband and three children.

"**Y**ears ago, my husband and I took a trip to Italy for Valentine's Day. I was trying on shoes without my husband, and noticed a man watching me. When I decided not to buy a particular pair he told the clerk he wanted to buy them for me!

Jeanie Schottenstein, Shoe Lover & Jay's Wife, DSW

I was so freaked out I called Jay and asked him to meet me at the store. When he arrived he asked me what happened. I told him and he asked, 'Where are the shoes?' I told him I put them back. He said,

'ARE YOU CRAZY? TAKE THE SHOES!'"